LAOZI'S *"DAODEJING"*

LAOZI'S *"DAODEJING"*

A NEW TRANSLATION WITH ENVIRONMENTALIST COMMENTARY

STEVE HALLETT

PURDUE UNIVERSITY PRESS

WEST LAFAYETTE, INDIANA

Cataloging-in-Publication Data on file at the Library Congress.
978-1-62671-268-3 (paperback)
978-1-62671-270-6 (epdf)
978-1-62671-269-0 (epub)

All photographs (Nikon Coolpix or iPhone) and all drawings (pencil), and paintings (black ink, brush on paper) by the author.

Cover images: White background of watercolor paper courtesy of xamtiw/iStock via Getty Images Plus. Heron ink painting created by the author.

To all my family

CONTENTS

ACKNOWLEDGMENTS

This book has been written over many years of largely solitary study, so the most important thanks go to my wife, Shelley, who puts up with my oddness with great patience and equanimity. Thanks to the many people with whom I have discussed various concepts developed here, particularly Shelley, Dan, Pat, Sami, and Chris, each of whom has given me valuable insights. Great thanks to my friends and colleagues Andrew Flachs and Yiwei Huang for thoughtful critiques and valuable editorial comments on the manuscript. Huge thanks to all the wonderful people at Purdue University Press, especially Neal Novak.

INTRODUCTION

I drift about like a desolate ocean. I blow around like a feckless wind.
I am not like other people. I am nourished by the great mother. (v. 20)

LAOZI AND THE *DAODEJING*

There is reason to believe that there was actually a man living around 600–400 BCE who was the originator of the book known as the *Daodejing*. The consistency of style and the coherence of message of the *Daodejing* seem to indicate a single author. On the other hand, it is probably more reasonable to believe that no such man existed and that the *Daodejing* is a compilation of sayings passed down through generations of oral history. It is also possible that the *Daodejing* emerged from offshoots of a range of philosophical schools such as those of Kongzi (Confucius, 551–479 BCE) and Mengzi (Mencius, 372–289 BCE) and might be best understood as a hybrid of ancient wisdoms.

Records of the life of Laozi are scant, and the most likely record comes from the great Han dynasty court historian Sima Qian (sometimes called the Herodotus of Chinese history),[1] who places Laozi in Quren village (present-day Liyi) and Chu State (present-day Henan Province) on the North China Plain during the Zhou dynasty. Laozi's given name, according to Sima Qian, was Li Er, but he has since been known or deified as Lao Er, Lao Jun, Tai-Shang Lao Jun, Lao Dun, Lao Dan, Tai-Shang Xuanyuan Huangdi, and Laozi (Lao Zi, Lao-Tzu, Lao-Tse). The name "Laozi" means "old master" or "old child."

Sima Qian mentions Laozi in a story about Confucius. According to the account, Confucius once visited with Laozi (his elder) but struggled to grasp his wisdom. Confucius said, "I know birds can fly. I know fishes can swim. I know wild animals can run. . . . As to the dragon, I cannot know how he can bestride the wind and clouds when he rises heavenward. Today I met Laozi. Is he like the dragon?"

But we cannot possibly trust this record. Sima Qian was writing at least four centuries after the lifetime of the presumed man and was relying on oral histories and scattered accounts that we should consider vulnerable to bias.

So, did a man called Laozi write the *Daodejing*? Probably not, not in the form in which we receive it, but I choose to embrace the idea of Laozi as representing the first in a line of great theorists whose work became one of the world's great philosophies and, having embraced him and linked him to the *Daodejing*, let's indulge ourselves by recounting the most famous story of his life, improbable (mythic) though it is.

Laozi had had enough. After many years of dedicated service as historian to the Zhou court trying to mitigate the follies of leaders and guide people on the Path, Dao, and teach them Virtue, De, he dropped everything and left. He clambered onto the back of a water buffalo and headed west. To this point he had been too humble to write down his wisdoms, but when he reached the western gate of the kingdom at the Xiangu Pass, he was begged to do exactly that by the border guard, Yinxi. What he wrote, so legend tells, in an outpouring of literary genius, were the five thousand or so characters that make up the two books of the *Daodejing*. And then he passed through the gate, into the West and was never heard from again—except through the voices, brushes, quills, and pens of millions of Daoists, Buddhists, mystics, scholars, and regular folk who still link his wisdoms from ancient China to the whole world.

A transcription and commentary of the *Daodejing* from scholar Wang Bi was used almost exclusively from his writing (approx. 226–249 CE) to the modern era. In 1973 two complete copies of the *Daodejing*, written on silk, were discovered at Mawangdui (Changsha, Hunan) and dated to 168 BCE.[2] Interestingly, the Mawangdui texts placed the De verses (normally verses 38–81) prior to the Dao verses (normally verses 1–37), which prompted Robert Henricks, a prominent scholar of the *Daodejing*, to title his translation the *Te-Tao Ching* (*De Dao Jing*). And then in 1993, scholars realized that the *Daodejing* was likely every bit as old as legend had told. Eight hundred bamboo slips marked with about two thousand characters from the *Daodejing* were excavated from a tomb in Guodian village (Jingmen, Hubei) and dated prior to 300 BCE.[3] The Guodian find confirmed that at least some of the *Daodejing* is more than 2,300 years old, within three centuries of the oldest legendary age of Laozi. The high level of fidelity found among copies of the *Daodejing* from 300 BCE, 168 BCE, and other very old texts shows that we have a document that has been passed down through the ages remarkably intact.

This high level of fidelity, it should be noted, pertains to the transcription of the characters, not their interpretation. The *Daodejing* was first written down in seal script (*zhuan shu*) and then clerical script (*li shu*) before finding its way into the relatively modern traditional and simplified characters (*kai shu*). The transcriptions from Chinese to Chinese appear to have been done faithfully, even as interpretation of the work has varied wildly. Translation into Western languages, however, has been fraught. How does one translate a text that is difficult to interpret in its original language? Well, one does one's best and risks criticism for misunderstanding, misinterpretation, Westernization, orientalism, and cultural appropriation.

Daoism has had an interesting journey through the centuries and the world. It has been adopted as both a philosophy (*daojia*) and a religion (Daojiao).[4] While Laozi is universally regarded as its most important author, the canon has been expanded by many other people. Some groups and their writings have tended to deify Laozi and apply his ideas religiously—as a path to the attainment of immortality, for example. This doesn't interest me much. Other groups and authors have resisted these urges and have studied Daoism in a strictly philosophical light. Prominent among them was Zhuangzi, who wrote the wonderful (and wonderfully humorous) book usually known as *The Zhuangzi*, which expounds the philosophy through tales and parables. The goal of the philosophical schools has been to use the principles of Daoism to understand the nature of the mind, people, and communities and to locate these within the larger workings of the cosmos.

One of the more fascinating aspects of the history of Daoism might be its intermingling with Buddhism. The two philosophies probably emerged independently around the same time, the one in China and the other in India, and they probably met when Buddhism moved into China along the southern branch of the Silk Road. Buddhism was undergoing its own evolution, with what is now known as Theravada Buddhism moving south into the rest of India and Southeast Asia and Mahayana Buddhism moving northward into China. In China, the mingling of Mahayana Buddhism with Daoism is generally considered to have resulted in Chan Buddhism, which reached its full flourishing centuries later in Japan, as Zen Buddhism. It is in its Zen iteration that the key tenets of Buddhism and Daoism are best known in the West.[5]

A PHILOSOPHY FOR PEOPLE
AND THE PLANET

What humans have achieved is remarkable. Our drive and persistence and our genius for technology have enabled us to subdue a perilous world and safeguard access to a huge share of its resources. Today, we can live in great comfort with abundant resources and pleasures. We have surely built the world of our dreams.

But no. We have damaged many beautiful places, extincted many species, and put the ecology of the planet out of balance.

Our desire to shape and control the world led us from fire, oxen, and the waterwheel to coal, oil, and natural gas. Our profligate use of fossil fuels has spilled greenhouse gases into the atmosphere and warmed the planet. Craving material comforts, we have commandeered resources, destroyed ecosystems, and littered the landscape with plastics and pollutants. And we have covered nearly every scrap of habitable land with cities and farms. Humans and our livestock now represent the vast majority of mammals on the planet. Nearly half the birds on Earth live and die on a poultry farm. We have reached the peak of civilization, at the height of our powers, and we can now look out over this human-made world and see what we have created. Not a dream, but a nightmare.

So, where to from here? The conventional wisdom sees a few ways forward. The first is through technology. If fossil fuels are filling the atmosphere with greenhouse gases, we must find new noncombustible forms of energy: sleeker wind turbines and better solar photovoltaics, perhaps, or tidal power plants or nuclear fusion. If plastics are trashing the planet, surely we can replace them with better materials: corn- or soybean-based products, perhaps, or gentler, greener biodegradable plastics. And if our agriculture is splayed over the landscape, surely we can find better ways of producing food: in hydroponic container farms and optimized fish farms, perhaps, or with lab-cultivated meats. And all of these solutions should be made as efficient as possible. We can produce more energy, materials, and food with less waste.

This is the technologist's vision. Technology might have gotten us into this mess, but this is because it was clunky and primitive. If we can make it better, cleaner, and more efficient, it will give us the control and comfort we want while protecting the environment. Technology isn't good enough yet, but it can be, and when it is, it will enable us to set nature free again. We need to keep innovating, say the technologists.

A second conventional wisdom is that our political and economic systems are to blame. Great problems assail us, but great solutions are possible, and a better politics would be able to unleash our collective wisdom. Solutions to our global crises are available or within reach, both technologically and socially, and if we could come together in common cause to enact them, we could save the world.

A third conventional wisdom is that everything is urgent. We need to stop climate change immediately, and if we don't it will be too late. If we let the climate system pass this threshold or that threshold, we'll never get it back under control. We also need to save Earth's biodiversity now before more species are lost. Bulldozers and chainsaws are slicing their way through tropical forests in a dozen countries even as we speak. They must be stopped now. And our landfills are overflowing with plastic toys, our oceans are littered with plastic bags, and our bodies are riddled with microplastics. We need to stop this madness within ten years, this generation, yesterday, immediately, urgently, now.

The technologies that have spawned our ecological impacts are modern, the political and economic systems that frustrate us are recent, our scientific understanding of world ecology and climate change is cutting-edge, and the anxiety to find technical and social solutions quickly is urgent and palpable. This all gives the impression that our problems are new. It feels as though we are living through a strange, temporary glitch in the history of the world. We have gone too far with our advanced technologies, and we have imperiled ourselves. We have put the world out of balance in short order, and we need to restore that balance in short order too. We have a modern crisis on our hands, but we can and will fix it, and we can and will get back on track.

There are a few problems with these ways of looking at things. The rapid accelerations we have seen in energy use, technology development, and greenhouse gas emissions did all occur in little more than a century. Graphs of these phenomena have been described as "hockey sticks" because of their sudden and explosive growth. And it is clearly no coincidence that the negative impacts map so closely to fossil fuel use. Our adoption of fossil fuels did nothing less than change the thermodynamics of civilization. This much, then, is modern and could be addressed by quitting fossil fuels.

But there's something more fundamental than fossil fuels. It wasn't by chance and accident that we started using fossil fuels when we did. The world was already in an age of accelerations brought on by colonialism and capitalism.

We can think of the world as having pools of resources linked by flows. The easiest image is pools of water: oceans, lakes, underground aquifers, ice sheets, glaciers, clouds, and water vapor linked by flows: streams, rivers, evaporation, and condensation. Another easy image is carbon, which can flow from an oil well to a gas tank to the atmosphere to a tree to a book. Ecology is a network of pools and flows.

Capital is a pool of wealth. It can flow among pools and can be used to access other pools. It can be used to collect water or harvest trees. Capitalism is therefore not just an economic system but also an integral part of the ecology of the modern world—a world ecology. It is a way of organizing nature. Whoever controls capital can control seams of coal, forests, or oceans of fish. And since capitalism is a human system, it is, at least in theory, ours to control. We can make it more expensive for a seam of coal to be mined. We can prevent a forest from being logged. Much, then, could be addressed by quitting or fixing capitalism.

But there are things more fundamental than capitalism.

Perhaps the most remarkable thing about our amazing, fast-paced, modern world is that it doesn't seem to have made us happier or wiser. We're still vying for more and more control over nature. Shouldn't it be obvious by now that there is no end to this struggle? The more control you have, the more control you need. And we're still vying for control over each other. Shouldn't it be obvious by now that we are at our best and happiest not when we compete but instead when we cooperate? We do understand this, some of us, some of the time, and we make progress, but then we regress. We say that we want to save the world, but we act otherwise. We say that we want to help others, but we act selfishly. How strange it is to realize that although our world may be more modern, we are still the same befuddled, dissatisfied, anxious strivers we were millennia ago. There seem to be fundamental flaws in the ways of people.

The wise among us have pondered this for millennia, and one of the wisest was Laozi. He pondered the relationship of people with the natural world, thought deeply about the dynamics of societies, and studied the human behaviors that mitigate competition and promote cooperation. He reached the insight that everything about people, from their relationships to each other to their relationships with the natural world, was dependent on their relationship with their own mind. The *Daodejing* offers us a philosophy that foregrounds balance, the relinquishment of control, the benefits of softness and flexibility, and the wisdom of nature's rhythms and flows. It is gently radical and radically gentle.

A RADICALLY GENTLE PHILOSOPHY

The *Daodejing* is a thoroughly unassuming book. It contains only about five thousand Chinese characters and translates to a mere five thousand to fifteen thousand words in English. At first blush, it seems like little more than a random collection of Hallmark card aphorisms (which is what many of its phrases have become), but beneath its apparent simplicity, the *Daodejing* has hidden depths, and the deeper you dig the more profound it becomes. Its themes are neither as random or scattered as they first seem but instead accumulate to expound one of the world's great philosophies. The following is a quick primer on some of its key concepts.

Dao (figure I.1) is the leading character in the doublet *Daode* (*Dao De*) in the title and the central concept of the *Daodejing*. So, what does it mean? Well, I'll explain it as best I can, but it means something slightly different to everyone, as Laozi warns in the very first phrase: *The Path that can be trodden is not the Eternal Path. The name that can be named is not the eternal name* (v. 1).

The first meaning of Dao is straightforward. It means "way" or "path" and can be used for a road or a lane, but it can also mean a moral path or ethical way. Dao also shows up in Chinese-derived languages. Kendo (*ken-dao*) is the Japanese "Way of the Sword,"

Dao

and taekwondo (*tae-kwon-dao*) is the Korean "Way of Kick and Punch." This aspect of the Dao is quite simple. The Dao suggests the paths you should tread in life, and many verses in the *Daodejing* point in the right direction:

> *It only takes the least scrap of sense to stay on the broad Path.* (v. 53)
>
> *Governing a big country is like cooking a small fish. Govern in accordance with the Dao.* (v. 60)
>
> *Dao is the refuge of all things. Treasure for the noble; protection for the wicked. . . . Thus is the Dao the gift of the world.* (v. 62)
>
> *The Way of heaven is to help without harming.* (v. 81)

But the Dao also has a larger meaning. Dao is the Way or Path of nature and natural cycles, of life and living things, of the cosmos, and represents the culmination of Laozi's spiritual questing. Dao is everything and how everything "works." One could translate Dao as "god" or "logos" in the purest sense, but such words are heavily freighted and carry secondary meanings that lead away from the Dao. The only way to zero in on what Laozi means by Dao is to study the *Daodejing*:

> *The Dao is an empty vessel that cannot be drained. . . . I do not know whose child it is. It seems like the ancestor of god.* (v. 4)

Call it the formless form; the imageless image; the unthought thought. (v. 14)

The Dao is eternally nameless; the uncarved block; minuscule, and yet beyond the scope of heaven and earth. (v. 32)

The Path maintains eternal nonaction and yet leaves nothing undone. (v. 37)

The motion of the Path is circular. The method of the Path is yielding. (v. 40)

Heaven's Path doesn't strive and yet ably wins, doesn't speak but answers fully, doesn't call and yet responds, doesn't rush but plans calmly. (v. 73)

The Way of heaven is like a stretched bow. Its higher tip is bent down. Its lower tip is bent up. It takes from what has too much and gives to what has too little. (v. 77)

So, Laozi presents a range of meanings of Dao, from simple suggestions about a way to live to descriptive pointings toward a cosmic and spiritual Path: a larger eternal Dao. The more carefully you look, the more you will see. Note that I sometimes translate Dao as "Path" or "Way" but more often just leave it as Dao so you can choose your own interpretation.

The first thing to know about De (figure I.2) is that although it's a fine thing, it's not quite Dao: *Lacking Dao we fall back on De. Lacking De we fall back on kindness. Lacking kindness, we fall back on morality. Lacking morals, we resort to rituals and rules* (v. 38). Laozi dislikes rituals and rules and finds morals to be often misguided. De is superior to kindness. Dao is superior to De, but it is through De that we get into the nitty-gritty of Laozi's life and leadership advice. Dao always sits on a higher plane as the Path—the True North, if you will—but De offers the road map.

De

There is some awkwardness to the interpretation of De, some of which stems from its ancient origins. De has a longer known lineage than Dao and is prominent in the Oracle Bones, which were inscriptions on ox scapulae, turtle plastrons, and the like, linked to the kings of the ancient (virtually mythic) Shang dynasty.[6] Some of the Oracle Bones are dated as far back as 1200 BCE. De was considered to be that special psychic quality of a king that conferred approval from spirit ancestors. It was a magical quality that was renewed with the birth of a new dynasty and could decline as a dynasty aged, fell into decadence, and veered toward collapse or revolution. Kings needed to protect and enhance their De in order to verify their legitimacy and protect their position. De was therefore both spiritual and a form of energy, perhaps best imagined as a spirit-energy that deified rulers and legitimized their mandate over the people. Thus, De is understood to have a moral dimension and to represent a psychic force. This resonates poorly in modern secular societies, and some of the clunkiness of Laozi's politics presumably stems from inheriting some of these ideas about mythic, spirit-enhanced leaders.

De is tricky to translate, and each translation leaves us with a clunky phrase or an English word lacking depth. Some options are "power," "the workings of," "bounty," "gratitude," "to be grateful for," "manifestation," and "quality." Previous authors have used a range of different translations in different verses, and the translation of De even varies in the titles of translations: Arthur Waley, *The Way and its Power*, and Stanislas Julien, *Lau-Tseu Tao-Te-King: Le Livre de la Voie et de la Vertu* (The Book of the Way and of Virtue).

I have translated De almost exclusively as virtue but not without trepidation. Virtue does not capture the meaning as well as I would prefer and risks diverting the mind to thoughts of "virtuous maidens" and the like, which could invoke the opposite of the intended meaning. I understand virtue as superior morals and ethics grounded in the Dao and guided by respect for the concepts of balance (yin-yang), nonaction (*wuwei*), the uncarved block (*pu*), the spontaneity of nature (*ziran*), and resisting cravings and desires (*yu*). De represents the virtuous, ethical, and quality-creating behaviors of wise people and the cogs, wheels, and motivating power of the Dao:

> *To give birth and nurture; to bear without possessing; to act without claiming; to lead*
>   *without dominating: this is profound virtue.* (v. 10)
> *Great virtue only comes from following the Path.* (v. 21)
> *Be the mountain stream[;] . . . your virtue is secure. Be an example[;] . . . your virtue will*
>   *not fail. Be the river valley[;] . . . your virtue will be inexhaustible.* (v. 28)
> *True virtue is higher than virtue; unassuming, and therefore virtuous. Fake virtue*
>   *is simply for display and therefore not virtuous at all. The most virtuous observe*
>   *nonaction and are unselfish. The less virtuous make sure they are seen to act.* (v. 38)

The wise ... treat good people well [and] ... treat bad people well. Thus, they have the
  virtue of goodness. They are trusting of people who are honest and also ... dishonest.
  Thus, they have the virtue of faithfulness. (v. 49)

To raise without possessing. To nourish without spoiling. To guide without controlling.
  This is the Primal De. (v. 51)

Cultivate yourself to develop genuine virtue ...—your family[,] ... the country[,] ... the
  world—to sustain universal virtue. (v. 54)

To fully embody virtue, be like a newborn. (v. 55)

Live sparingly and flexibly. This is what it is to accumulate virtue. With abundant virtue,
  everything can be overcome, anything can be achieved, and you are fit to rule. (v. 59)

To big or small, to many or few, speak to vice with virtue. (v. 63)

It is virtue to attend to you own obligations. It is not virtue to insist others do the
  same. (v. 79)

The characters yin and yang (figure I.3) are not found frequently in the *Daodejing*, but the ideas they convey are central. Yin and yang teach us to seek balance. Yang represents the flashy, material, tough things: the masculine,[7] the strong, the hard, activity, heat, the higher place, white, and bright light on the sunny side of the mountain. Yin represents the gentle, intangible, forgiving things: the feminine, the yielding, the flexible, passivity, cold, the lower place, black, and the darkness on shaded side of the mountain. Yin and yang are represented in the *Taiji* symbol (see the illustration for verse 2) in which a white teardrop and a black teardrop shape wrap around each other, or chase

Yin and Yang

each other, in a circle. Each shape has an eye of the opposite color representing the nucleus of an impending phase change. Imagined as a dynamic thing, the teardrop shapes constantly switch places and colors. Yin and yang are not opposing forces but are instead complements: parts of a whole. *Thirty spokes join at the hub but the axle turns in its empty space.... What is present makes a thing valuable. What is absent makes it work* (v. 11). If it is to turn, the wheel requires both the solid yang axle, a material thing, and the empty yin space, an immaterial thing.

The *Daodejing* speaks frequently about the dangers of polarized thinking and advocates balance as a guiding principle. *Be equally wary of honor and disgrace* (v. 13). We do not need to be told to avoid disgrace. It is a painful emotion suffered by our strangely social species. Laozi, however, warns us to be equally wary of honor in an ancient Chinese iteration of "Pride cometh before a fall." Honor and disgrace are yin and yang, and if you navigate a balanced path between them, resisting the cravings for glory and honor, you are much less likely to suffer disgrace.

In seeking balance, Laozi repeatedly guides us toward yin. This is not because yin is superior to yang but instead because it is underappreciated. Consider the leaders we choose. We know, when we properly engage our brains and analyze the data, that women are better suited for leadership than men. I'm making huge "in the aggregate" generalizations here, of course, but women tend to be more flexible, deliberative, and collaborative. More yin. Isn't that what we should want in leaders? The leaders we more often choose are strong, decisive, and self-assured. Men. Yang. I think that Laozi would be impressed by New Zealand's Jacinda Ardern and Finland's Sanna Marin. Compare their approaches to the COVID-19 pandemic with those of Britain's Boris Johnson and America's Donald Trump. *Know the masculine but cleave to the feminine.... Know the light but cleave to the dark.... Know your honor but cleave to your humility* (v. 28).

The balance of yin and yang comes less from the fact that they are opposite sides of the same coin than from the fact that they represent essential parts of the same coin. A coin is not a coin unless it is a flat disk with two sides and the two sides are made at the same time. *Existence and nonexistence arise together* (v. 2). The cosmos is made of protons and electrons, matter and antimatter, yin and yang.

Wuwei (figure I.4), or *wei wuwei*, has a few meanings. First, it means "do not do," which is better understood by phrasing it "do not–do." A little mental gymnastics is required here. Think of not-do as an action: as something you do. *Wei wuwei* is the act of not-doing, not acting, not interfering, trying to not control, showing restraint. It is not laziness. Laziness has you not-doing for all the wrong reasons. *Wuwei* has you not-doing for all the right reasons. Don't fuss with it. Stop meddling. As Aldo Leopold said of nature in *A Sand County Almanac,* "The first law of intelligent tinkering is to keep all the pieces," which, since you never can keep all the pieces, means "Don't meddle with the environment."[8]

Wuwei

An extension of this meaning is the advice to resist acting too quickly or reacting to things rashly. A *wuwei* approach is one that takes the time to weigh up the best possible course of action. Ideally, action will be avoided or restrained. Act, don't react, might be a suitable mantra (see v. 64).

Laozi repeatedly advises us to not-do:

The wise govern by . . . practicing not-doing to maintain balance. (v. 3)

Do good work and then step back. (v. 9)

"Who by nothing but stillness can render muddy water clear? (v. 15)

The softest things in the world override the hardest. The formless infiltrate the
impenetrable. Thus, we understand the influence of doing not-doing; of teaching
without telling. (v. 43)

Movement overcomes cold. Stillness overcomes heat. Calmness keeps the world in
order. (v. 45)

Gain the world by not-doing. Try to control the world and it will evade you. (v. 48)

Use not-doing in dealing with the natural world. (v. 57)

Do without doing. Act without acting. . . . Tackle the difficult in its simplest form. Tackle
big problems while they are small. (v. 63)

Hard and stiff belong to death and tender and gentle belong to life. Thus is the unyielding
army shattered and the unbending tree splintered. (v. 76)

An additional meaning of *wuwei* is to not force or to not struggle, and this meaning is used in reference to the skilled, effortless, beautiful, often unconscious action we refer to as "flow," or being "in the zone." If you must act, act with beauty. Build with quality. Work with skill:

When the great leader has done her work the people will say, "Look! We did it all
ourselves!" (v. 17)
A skilled tracker leaves no trace. A skilled speaker leaves no doubt. A skilled bookkeeper
needs no gadgets. (v. 27)
This is the secret insight, how the soft and weak defeat the hard and strong. (v. 36)
The Path maintains eternal nonaction and yet leaves nothing undone. (v. 37)
Those who act cause harm. Those who snatch fumble. (v. 64)

Pu (figure I.5) is the ultimate image of *wuwei*, and I translate it almost exclusively
as "the uncarved block." Notice that the Chinese character is an ideogram of trees. *Pu*
can also be used more generally to indicate anything in its pure, untrammeled state. The
classic image of *Pu* is an uncarved block of jade, which offers many possibilities to the
skilled sculptor. Great beauty can be revealed by carving away surplus material from a
block of jade. Once carved, however, and a particular form revealed, the block of jade's
potential to reveal other forms has been removed.

Pu

The *Daodejing* invokes us to be like the uncarved block, simple, uncluttered, un-adorned, in our natural state, and full of potential:

> *The ancient masters were . . . sincere and uncomplicated like the uncarved block.* (v. 15)
> *Be simple; like undyed silk; like the uncarved block.* (v. 19)
> *The uncarved block can be shaped into useful things. The wise are turned into leaders without any carving.* (v. 28)
> *The nameless uncarved block tempers desire.* (v. 37)
> *Don't desire to be precious, like jade. Be tough, like common stone.* (v. 39)

The ultimate uncarved block is nature: the cosmos, the Dao. The *Daodejing* repeat-edly reminds us that everything is cyclic—*The motion of the Path is circular. The method of the Path is yielding. Everything is born of being except being* (v. 40)—and imperma-nent—*A flower grows, blooms, returns to the root* (v. 16)—and in its most beautiful state when cycling naturally through its births and deaths following the Dao: *The Dao is eter-nally nameless: the uncarved block* (v. 32).

Ziran (figure I.6) basically means "nature," or "natural," and is interesting because it is made from the characters *zi*, meaning "self," and *ran*, meaning "right." Nature therefore makes itself right or is self-right or self-so. One fascinating translation of *ziran* comes from the end of verse 35 where Laozi says *Dao fa ziran*, which could simply mean that "Dao emulates nature" or could be rendered as "Dao is self-so," which I like, but the versatility of *ziran* enables a bolder interpretation: "The Dao simply is." The *Daode-jing* urges us to examine the workings of nature as a guide to living a good life. Nature is a manifestation of the Dao, and we are one of nature's manifestations. Laozi conjures natural features and processes such as water to evoke natural flows through landscapes and through plants to evoke natural flows through seasons and generations. A philos-ophy of *ziran* is uncontrived and spontaneous:

Ziran

欲

Yu

The space between heaven and earth is a bellows. Empty and yet inexhaustible. The more it is pumped the more it produces. (v. 5)

The highest good is like water. . . . It settles in the lowest places. This is how it shows us the Path. (v. 8)

Returning to the root is peaceful; a return to one's own nature. (v. 16)

Nature is not a blabbermouth: a storm doesn't go on all morning. (v. 23)

The *Daodejing* offers some simple and direct advice in achieving De, virtue, and finding the Path, Dao. Seek balance: yin-yang, do not-doing: *wei wuwei*, emulate nature, *ziran*, and be like the uncarved block, *pu*. But how? Laozi counsels us to temper our cravings and desires, which is expressed with a number of images, phrases, and words, one of which is *yu* (figure I.7).

The idea conveyed by *yu* is similar to the Buddhist concept of *Tanha*, which is central to the Four Noble Truths. Much mental suffering, particularly the constant dissatisfactions, wranglings, and disappointments of life that can lock us in perpetual low-grade misery, can be attributed to *yu*. Temper desires and cravings—lower needs and expectations—and contentedness will thrive.

The Buddha expressed this in a simple story. Consider the phrase "I want happiness." Now, remove the "I," which is the ego, the self. Now remove the "want," which is the cravings and desires, the *tanha*, the *yu*, and what do you have left? You're left with "happiness." Laozi expressed this in many different images:

Tempering desire, you see the depths. Embracing desire, you see the surfaces. (v. 1)
Be simple.... The self recedes. Desires soften. (v. 19)
The great Way is wide; in flood.... It has no needs; no desires. (v. 34)
With desire managed all is quiet. The world settles into peace. (v. 37)
Don't desire to be precious, like jade. Be tough, like common stone. (v. 39)
The greatest mistake is desire.... The greatest curse is craving. (v. 46)
The wise do not desire desire nor treasure treasures. (v. 64)

TRANSLATION AND INTERPRETATION

The *Daodejing* cannot be translated in a way that will please everybody—a fact that is made obvious by the existence of hundreds of translations, no two of which are the same. Indeed, some translations bear precious little resemblance to each other.

Chinese lacks linguistic inflection, making a number of grammatical categories malleable, including tense, gender, and number. The first copies of the *Daodejing* were presumably written in the now obsolete seal script. Add to this that the document is delivered in a very sparse style leaving much open to interpretation, and it becomes clear that the text cannot be translated definitively. Indeed, a word-by-word transliteration into English renders a fairly meaningless word salad that is useful for scholars but unreadable. Choices must be made.

The translation of any document must be performed as faithfully as possible, but with faithfulness to which principles? The literal meaning of each character, line, stanza, and verse is important, but so too are the intended meanings if they can be deciphered. The tenor and mood of the document must also be captured if they can be discerned. Alas, we cannot be completely faithful to all these demands and must strike a balance.

We are confronted with dilemmas in the very first line of the document (figure I.8). What does the first line of the *Daodejing* mean? Well, as a translator, it means you're already in trouble.

dào kě dào fēi cháng dào   道 可 道 非 常 道

Figure I.8

Word-for-word translations offer the following range of possible meanings for each character, but the best choice of word is dependent on how we interpret the context.

Dao   Tao, path, way, road, nature, the absolute, reason, spoken, told, talked of, trodden, walked

ke   can, can be, able to, becomes

fei   not, cannot, opposes, other than, not the same as

chang   always, fixed, eternal, the eternal, absolute, constant, unchanging

Since there is a range of possible transliterations for each character in the first line, there are a number of possible representations of the phrase. Here is how a number of different authors have presented the first line:

ADDISS AND LOMBARDO: "Tao called Tao is not Tao."

ABBOTT: "The way possible to think runs counter to the constant way."

BYNNER: "Existence is beyond the power of words to define."

CARUS: "The reason that can be reasoned is not the eternal reason."

FENG AND ENGLISH: "The Tao that can be told is not the eternal Tao."

HENRICKS: "As for the Way, the Way that can be spoken is not the constant Way."

HOGAN: "If you can talk about it, it ain't Tao."

HUANG: "A tao that can be spoken about is not the constant tao."

JULIEN: "La voie qui peut être exprimée par la parole n'est pas la voie éternelle."

LAU: "The way that can be spoken of is not the constant way."

LEGGE: "The Tao that can be trodden is not the enduring and unchanging Tao."

LE GUIN: "The way you can go isn't the real way."

MITCHELL: "The Tao that can be told is not the eternal Tao."

PEPPER AND WANG: "The Dao that can be spoken is not the eternal Dao."

STAR: "A way that can be walked is not The Way."

STENNUD: "The Way that can be walked is not the eternal Way."

WALEY: "The Way that can be told is not an Unvarying Way."

WILSON: "The way that can be articulately described is not the unchanging way."

[HALLETT]: *The path that can be trodden is not the eternal Path* (v. 1).

Some phrases and verses are particularly difficult to translate. Verse 71 is the one I find to be the most opaque (figure I.9). Even if you are unable to read Chinese you can easily see that this verse uses frequent repeats of a very few characters. A direct transliteration could be made as follows:

汭1 七十一

zhī bù zhī shàng bù zhī zhī bìng	知不知上不知知病
fú wéi bìng bìng shì yǐ bù bìng	夫唯病病是以不病
shèng rén bù bìng yǐ qí bìng bìng	圣人不病以其病病
fú wéi bìng bìng shì yǐ bù bìng	夫唯病病是以不病

Figure I.9

Know not know better not know know sickness
So only sickness sickness therefore not sickness
Wise man not sickness because he sickness sickness
So only sickness sickness therefore not sickness

How do we make sense of this? In place of "sickness" we could use "sick," "disease," or more general words such as "defect." The phrases "Know not know" and "Not know know" in the first two lines are generally interpreted the same way to mean "To know that you don't know" and "To not know what you know," but there are multiple interpretations, and who is to say which is the "right" one? Here is my translation:

To know your ignorance is good
To be ignorant of your ignorance is a sickness

To be sick of sickness is healthy

The wise see sickness for what it is
and so they are healthy

This is most definitely not a transliteration. It is arguably not even a translation, and it's riddled with intuition and interpretation.

Another problem of opaque language is seen in verse 60 (figure I.10), where I have not only interpreted the meaning of the text but have also had to modify its content in order to render it into English in a way that links it to what I perceive to be the meaning of the verse as a whole. I hate to do this, and this is one of the very few places I have done so. My interpretation may not accurately represent Laozi's intent at all, but it's the best I can do.

fēi qí shén bù shāng rén	非 其 神 不 伤 人
shèng rén yì bù shāng rén	圣 人 亦 不 伤 人
fū liǎng bù xiāng shāng	夫 两 不 相 伤
gù dé jiāo guī yān	故 德 交 归 焉

Figure I.10

A fair transliteration might be as follows:

wrong his spirit not wound people
the sage also not wound people
man also not assist wound
hence virtue gives up returns to here

I render the phrase as follows:

If evil has no reason to flourish
and the wise have no reason to intervene
their virtues can converge and be unified

Last comes a few stock phrases that I have chosen to either modify or keep. Probably the most egregious modification I make is of *shengren*, "the sage." Most authors translate *Sheng ren* or *shengren* as "the sage" or "the wise man," but I have usually translated it as "the wise," declining to assign gender. I prefer this translation because it enables us to include the layperson and ourselves among the candidates for wisdom, and we can imagine "our wiser selves" in the reading. This was almost certainly not the intent of Laozi, writing *shengren* in first millennium BCE China. I've Westernized here. Please feel free to scratch out "the wise" in the text and replace it with "the sage."

I have left intact other stock phrases that are frequently translated. One example is "to stay with the baggage wagons," which appears to be a stock phrase meaning "to preserve one's dignity" but is treated differently by different translators (see v. 26). Unsure of its present-day meaning, I have left it alone. Maybe Laozi is simply reminding us that at the airport, "our baggage must be attended at all times."

Another stock phrase, found in a number of verses, is "the ten thousand things," which many authors translate as "all living things," "the whole of nature," or something similar. I think the reader can understand the meaning of "the ten thousand things" without having it spoon-fed to them, so this is my preference here.

The same is true for *pu*, the uncarved block. A metaphor as exquisite as this loses its power when explained. I explain it in the supporting text but not in the verses.

A second group of difficult decisions in translation concern style. The *Daodejing* is not a collection of poems per se, but it is beautifully poetic. It has a very clear meter and rhyme, which can be easily leveraged in Chinese, a language characterized by short syllables and many homophones. The following are some examples.

Verse 81 (figure I.11) uses repeating and reversing phrases. It looks lovely on the page and sounds lovely to the ear. My translation attempts to honor the meter, rhyme, and phrase reversals without sacrificing any meaning:

Truthful words are not pretty
Pretty words are not true

Good people are not argumentative
Contentious people are not good

Wise people are not learned
Learned people are not wise

xìn yán bù měi	信 言 不 美
měi yán bù xìn	美 言 不 信
shàn zhě bù biàn	善 者 不 辯
biàn zhě bù shàn	辯 者 不 善
zhī zhě bù bó	知 者 不 博
bó zhě bù zhī	博 者 不 知

Figure I.11

Verse 54 (figure I.12) has a lovely structure of internal repetition with the Chinese characters offering a fascinating visual structure on the page. I translate the repeating motifs as follows:

Cultivate yourself to develop genuine virtue
Cultivate your family to foster a wealth of virtue
Cultivate the village to support enduring virtue
Cultivate the country to promote abundant virtue
Cultivate the world to sustain universal virtue

xiū zhī yú shēn qí dé nǎi zhēn	修 之 于 身 其 德 乃 真
xiū zhī yú jiā qí dé nǎi yú	修 之 于 家 其 德 乃 余
xiū zhī yú xiāng qí dé nǎi cháng	修 之 于 乡 其 德 乃 长
xiū zhī yú bāng qí dé nǎi fēng	修 之 于 邦 其 德 乃 丰
xiū zhī yú tiān xià qí dé nǎi pǔ	修 之 于 天 下 其 德 乃 普

Figure I.12

Sometimes I get the distinct impression Laozi is just having fun with language. Is *buyu lulu ruyu* written for the meaning or the fun word sounds? It nails them both.

bu yu lu lu ru yu   Don't desire to be precious like jade
luo luo ru dan   Be tough like common stone

Another example comes from verse 63 (figures I.13, I.14, and I.14). The first two lines are about *wuwei* and represent core concerns of the Dao, but the third line is odd.

wéi wú wéi   为 无 为

Figure I.13

shì wú shì 事 无 事

Figure I.14

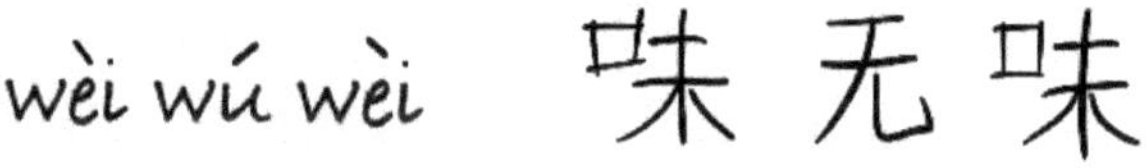

wèi wú wèi 味 无 味

Figure I.15

Act without acting
Teach without teaching
Find flavor in the bland

"Find flavor in the bland"? Perhaps the translation should be "Taste not taste" or "Flavor not flavor." I don't think it matters all that much. I think that the line is simply included for the *wei wu wei* homophone. If so, this line could never carry its original intent forward into English. It is just for yuks.

The final bias in translation comes from the morals and intent of the translator. Translators must keep themselves out of the way as much as possible and let the voice of the author ring true, but this objectivity can only ever be partial. Some will come to the *Daodejing* in search of practical advice on living a virtuous life or being an honorable leader and will emphasize those aspects. Others may come from a strictly literary standpoint, seeking accuracy above all else, or from a historical perspective, looking to compare and contrast the *Daodejing* with other texts of the same era. Many come from a contemplative point of view, looking to the *Daodejing* for spiritual growth. They too will find what they are looking for here and will likely reveal this in their translations. The *Daodejing* is so wonderfully broad and opaque that there is the danger that translators might find what they're looking for, whether it is here or not. My biases tend toward environmentalism, social justice, and the contemplative. These biases surely show through in the translations, although I have tried to limit them in the verses and use the essays to highlight them

I submit my English rendition of the *Daodejing* for your criticism. Where I have strayed too far from your understanding of Laozi's intended meaning or from an aesthetic that suits your ear, I apologize and welcome your corrections and suggestions.

I consulted dozens of translations. My favorites were those of Paul Carus, Ursula Le Guin, and Stephen Mitchell, but every translation taught me something. The ones I needed the most were those that gave transliterations and insight into accurate translation. The early translations (esp. Carus, Lau, Legge, and Waley) and the step-by-step transliterations (Abbott, Carus, Pepper and Wang, and Star) were essential resources. I couldn't have attempted this project without them. Other translations attempted different styles and different approaches. These were sometimes wonderful to my ear and sometimes discordant, but I learned from them all. Some translations stayed very close to Laozi's wording, perhaps losing some flow or elegance or seeming clunky in English, while others ventured further from the original wording—sometimes too far, in my opinion—in search of a desired style or interpretation. I am indebted to all the authors listed below whose work I ransacked to find my own meaning and to develop my own way to present Laozi's classic.

SOURCES CONSULTED

Abbott, Carl. *Tao Te Ching: Word for Word*. CreateSpace Independent Publishing Platform, 2012. This is a self-published book that I found at amazon.com. It has a number of really interesting and often quite personal commentaries on the Dao and life. The word-for-word transliteration was valuable and reliable. Some of the verse notes were also very enjoyable.

Addiss, Stephen, and Stanley Lambardo. *Lao-Tzu Tao Te Ching*. Hackett, 1993. This is a really nice, tidy, slim book with a very spare, unadorned, and effective translation—one of my favorite translations. It also has a short introduction and a few translation notes.

Bynner, Witter. *The Way of Life According to Lao Tzu: An American Version*. Capricorn Books, 1944. This is a fascinating version. To my ear, it makes the mistake of trying to convert ancient Chinese poetry into a Western poetic with a heavy meter and end rhyme. This doesn't work for me, but I learned from studying Bynner's approach.

Carus, Paul. *Lao-Tze's Tao-Te-King: Chinese-English with Introduction, Transliteration, and Notes*. Open Court Publishing Co., 1898. Carus's book is one of the most important translations and a valuable source of transliteration and history. It is one of the first accurate and effective translations, written at the end of the nineteenth century, and nearly all subsequent translations have relied on this work. It has been my Rosetta stone to the *Daodejing*. Carus's word-by-word transliterations were indispensable. I have spent hundreds of hours with this book over the last decade. Carus was convinced of the historicity of Laozi as a contemporary of Confucius and as the author of the *Daodejing*. Carus's translation uses poetic adornment only sparingly and is mostly delivered in prose. His book is highly readable and accessible. Carus set a high bar for translations of the *Daodejing* more than 125 years ago and has been surpassed only occasionally since. Of his approach to translation, Carus said, "The purpose of the present translation is first to bring the Tao-Teh-King within easy reach of everybody, and secondly to offer to the student of comparative religion a version which would be a faithful reproduction not only of the sense but of all the characteristic qualities, especially the terseness and the ruggedness of its style. . . . While linguistic obscurities have been removed as much as possible, the sense has not been rendered more definite than the original would warrant."

Chalmers, John. *The Speculations on Metaphysics, Polity, and Morality of the "Old Philospher" Lau-Tsze*. Trubner, 1868. A very enjoyable and very early English translation. Very informative footnotes and brief commentaries. The translations use a poetry and language that may have been very modern for their time and divert from transliteration in order to unravel explanations, but this translation seems cumbersome today. Nonetheless, it is a very valuable document.

Feng, Gia-Fu, and Jane English. *Lau Tsu Tao Te Ching: A New Translation*. Vintage Books, 1972. This is a really lovely book containing thoughtful and straightforward translations. It also contains simple photographs and calligraphy, which create a lovely ambience. A very Dao presentation of the *Daodejing*.

Henricks, Robert G. *Lao-Tzu Te-Tao Ching: A New Translation Based on the Recently Discovered Ma-wang-tui Texts*. Ballantine Books, 1989. After 2,500 years, suddenly two new versions of the *Daodejing*, written on silk, popped up near the village of Mawangdui. The silk was dated to 168 BCE. As with the next book on the list, analyzing the Guodian text, Henricks's book provides a deep dive into the new information, showing character-by-character differences. The book is an academic document that is very difficult to read but is an exciting primary source. Interestingly, the Mawangdui texts reversed the order of the two parts of the *Daodejing*, with verses 38–81 preceding verses 1–37, which is why Henricks calls his new version the *Te-Tao Ching*.

Henricks, Robert G. *Lao Tzu's Tao Te Ching: A Translation of the Startling New Documents Found at Guodian*. Columbia University Press, 2000. This book is another new discovery of a copy of the *Daodejing*—this one even older than the Mawangdui texts, written on bamboo slips and dated to 300 BCE. The Guodian document has some differences from the Mawangdui texts but is much more remarkable in its similarity than its differences. As with the previous book on the Mawangdui texts, Henricks's book provides a thorough analysis of the new information, showing character-by-character differences.

Hogan, Ron. *Getting Right with Tao: A Contemporary Spin on the Tao Te Ching*. Channel V Books, 2010). This is not a translation but is a fun interpretation with some good no-nonsense advice. I like this excerpt from verse 32: "Weapons are terrible things. If

you want to get right with Tao, reject weapons." That's a pretty good no-bullshit translation of the text. I also like this, from verse 42: "Chapter 42 starts out with some cosmic
mumbo-jumbo about Tao making one . . . Frankly, I wouldn't worry about it too much."

Huang, Chichung. *Tao Te Ching: A Literal Translation with an Introduction, Notes, and
Commentary.* Asian Humanities Press, 2003. This is a very useful text because the verses
are rendered quite literally, as the title promises, but this does make them much less readable and enjoyable in English. The book has extensive, valuable notes.

Julien, Stanislas. *Lao-Tseu Tao-Te-King: Le Livre de la Voie et de la Vertu.* L'Imprimerie
Royale, 1842. The first Western translation of the *Daodejing* was Julien's, in French. My
French isn't great, but it is good enough to see that Julien really captured Laozi's great
work here and set a really high bar with the first European translation. Paul Carus, the
author of the great 1898 translation, raved about the Julien translation, claiming to find
it indispensable. This 1842 translation is a gem.

Kreger, DW. *The Tao of Yoda: Based upon the Tao Te Ching by Lao Tzu.* Windham Ever-
itt, 2012. This little book is brilliant. Go through the *Daodejing* replacing "Dao" with
"Force" and "Wise" with "Jedi" and keep the original Chinese syntax, which sounds a
lot like how Yoda speaks, and you get verse 40. "In cycles, the force moves. In yielding,
the force is used."

Lau, D. C. *Lao Tzu Tao Te Ching.* Penguin, 1963. I relied on a number of sources from the
turn of the twentieth century and the turn of the twenty-first century. For the most part
the midcentury material that I came across was poetically contrived and less useful. Not
so with D. C. Lau. This is probably the first really good book from the later twentieth
century, and it seems to reset the scene for translations of the *Daodejing.* Lau's book has
detailed notes and an elegant, enjoyable translation.

Legge, James. *Lau Tzu Tao Te Ching.* Oxford University Press, 1891. This is one of the earliest English translations, written in a mixture of poetry and prose. I find the prose quite
pleasant to read, but the poetry uses a rather forced end rhyme style popular in the late
nineteenth century, and I find it clunky. The poetic style causes the translations to twist
into pretzels to find rhyming words where much better words are available. Nonetheless,
this is an important work and comes with very valuable commentaries and footnotes.

Le Guin, Ursula K. *Lao Tzu Tao Te Ching: A Book about the Way and the Power of the Way.*
Shambhala, 2019. Overall, I think this is my favorite translation. It is a very simple and
elegant book. Ursula Le Guin (1929–2018) was a wonderful and successful science fic-
tion writer and also a poet. Her handling of these translations is elegant without being
overly adorned and remain reasonably faithful to the text. There are also some pointed
and quirky footnotes.

Mitchell, Stephen. *Tao Te Ching: A New English Version.* Harper Perennial, 1988. To my
understanding, this is the best-selling translation of the *Daodejing.* Some people love
it, and others criticize it quite heavily. It is one of the most cavalier translations. There

are sections of some verses that Mitchell skips, and there are translations of some verses that are highly speculative. The obvious criticism is that this version may not be faithful enough to the original to warrant the name *translation*, but Mitchell doesn't call it a translation; he calls it a version. Splitting hairs, perhaps. On the positive side, the poetic style is really wonderful. The language is spare and simple and probably captures the linguistic music of the original Chinese better than any other English translation. Pick your poison. Personally, I love this book, but I couldn't use it to help my translations. Here is what Mitchell says about his approach: "With great poetry, the freest translation is sometimes the most faithful.... I have paraphrased, expanded, contracted, interpreted, worked with the text, played with it, until it became embodied in a language that felt genuine to me." Mitchell's book is the yin to Arthur Waley's yang.

Pepper, Jeff, and Xiao Hui Wang. *Daodejing in Clear English: Including a Step by Step Translation*. Imagin8 Press, 2019. Pepper and Wang appear to run their own business distributing English-Chinese books to help English speakers learn Chinese. This was a really useful book. The translations themselves are quite literal, which makes them a little difficult to interpret, but the step-by-step translations were easy to cross-check against other resources.

Star, Jonathan. *Tao Te Ching: The Definitive Edition*. Tarcher Penguin, 2001. This is a really wonderful book that provides very interesting translations, a detailed word-by-word translation, and numerous insights and commentaries. The translation was very useful to me as a point of contrast. Star tends to translate in a much longer form than the original in an attempt to clarify the meaning. This does not suit my sensibility, but I found it effective and useful. Star uses many more words in his translations than I do. His word-by-word translations are wonderful and provide multiple alternate translations.

Stennud, Stefan. *Tao Te Ching: The Taoism of Lao Tzu Explained*. Arriba, 2011. This is a really wonderful book in which the author gives his interpretations of each verse. The interpretations are often insightful, frequently amusing, and always valuable. The translations of the verses are also very effective: no-nonsense, clean, and well done.

Waley, Arthur. *The Way and its Power: Lao Tzu's Tao Te Ching and Its Place in Chinese Thought*. Grove Press, 1958. This is an excellent mid-twentieth-century translation that I really enjoyed. The translations use a fairly free poetic form with some prose. They are very close to the original, clunky at times but nonetheless quite readable. There are limited notes and footnotes, although they are valuable. There is a long, valuable introduction. Waley acknowledges that his renderings might be a little stodgy at times but defends his approach: "It seems to me that when the main importance of a work is its beauty, the translator must be prepared to sacrifice a great deal in the way of detailed accuracy in order to preserve in the translation the quality which gives the original its importance. Such a translation I call 'literary,' as opposed to 'philological.' I want to make it clear that this translation of the Tao-Te-Ching is not 'literary,' for the simple reason that the importance of the original lies not in its literary quality but in the things it says, and it has been my one aim to reproduce what the original says with detailed accuracy." Waley's book is the yang to Stephen Mitchell's yin.

Wilson, William S. *Tao Te Ching: A New Translation; Lao Tzu.* Shambhala, 2013. Wilson's book is quite enjoyable and has some very interesting extra notes on Zen and martial arts.

VERSE 1. IT'S ALL HERE

Dao character, the Way, Path, etc.

1 一

dào kě dào fēi cháng dào	道可道非常道	
míng kě míng fēi cháng míng	名可名非常名	
wú míng tiān dì zhī shǐ	无名天地之始	
yǒu míng wàn wù zhī mǔ	有名万物之母	
gù cháng wú yù yǐ guān qí miào	故常无欲以观其妙	
cháng yǒu yù yǐ guān qí jiǎo	常有欲以观其徼	
cǐ liǎng zhě tóng chū ér yì míng	此两者同出而异名	
tóng wèi zhī xuán	同谓之玄	
xuán zhī yòu xuán zhòng miào zhī mén	玄之又玄众妙之门	

The path that can be trodden is not the Eternal Path
The name that can be spoken is not the eternal name

Nameless it is the origins of the universe
Named it is the mother of the ten thousand things

Tempering desire you see the depths
Embracing desire you see the surfaces
    Different perspectives but of the same source

This unity is the deep mystery
    the mystery of mysteries
    and the gateway to spiritual awakening

The Dao is matter, it is energy, it is the animating force of the cosmos. The Dao was here before time, before the origins of the universe. It is the Way, the Path. Meanwhile, it is also a path people can follow to lead a better life.

The Dao is different things to different people and cannot easily be explained by one person to another. The Dao is whatever it is to you: a sense of wonder that you cannot quite grasp, ecological change, a forest growing back after fire, the coevolution of predator and prey, parasite and host. It is clouds forming, moving, rain falling. It is a limestone mountain eroding into the sea, coral polyps building the lime back into reefs, tectonic subduction lifting the reef and the seabed back into a mountain range. It is that sense of physics that you cannot derive mathematically: some function of gravity, space, time . . .

Whatever this obscure thing called the Dao might be, the *Daodejing* is its seminal text, and much of what the *Daodejing* might be able to teach us, unteach us, or make us curious about is promised here in the first verse.

First, the Path that we can walk and speak of is only our personal path, not *the* Path. We can try to name and teach it, but its nature can never be fully conveyed. What can be learned from the *Daodejing* intellectually can be taught, but what can be felt can only be pointed at. In its pristine, unnamed state the Dao is the huge, unknowable motivator of the universe. In its named state it is the lesser but still magnificent *mother of the ten thousand things*, which is to say everything that has physical form.

Second, the Path is a means of seeing how the world is processed and performed by our minds. Our minds shape and color our view of the world and introduce analysis, abstraction, bias, and many forms of mental suffering. Much suffering stems from cravings, prejudices, and lusts: what Laozi calls *desires*. Desires can be pretty fantastic, and living in a trivial surface world driven by desires is to *see the surfaces*. It is not all bad, for a while at least, but it creates mental suffering. To *see the depths* requires us to temper our desires.

Finally, this first verse of the *Daodejing* promises us that following the Dao can help us unify the world of surfaces with the world of depths. To the person who wishes to delve into their own mind and investigate the unity of these inner and outer worlds, the *Daodejing* can be the *gateway to a spiritual awakening*.

VERSE 2. YIN AND YANG

Taiji symbol representing yin and yang

2　二

tiān xià jiē zhī měi zhī wéi měi sī è yǐ	天 下 皆 知 美 之 为 美 斯 恶 已
jiē zhī shàn zhī wéi shàn sī bù shàn yǐ	皆 知 善 之 为 善 斯 不 善 已
gù yǒu wú xiāng shēng	故 有 无 相 生
nán yì xiāng chéng	难 易 相 成
cháng duǎn xiāng xíng	长 短 相 形
gāo xià xiāng qīng	高 下 相 倾
yīn shēng xiāng hé	音 声 相 和
qián hòu xiāng suí	前 后 相 随
shì yǐ shèng rén chǔ wú wéi zhī shì	是 以 圣 人 处 无 为 之 事
xíng bù yán zhī jiāo	行 不 言 之 教
wàn wù zuò yān ér bù cí	万 物 作 焉 而 不 辞
shēng ér bù yǒu	生 而 不 有
wéi ér bù shì	为 而 不 恃
gōng chéng ér fú jū	功 成 而 弗 居
fū wéi fú jū	夫 唯 弗 居
shì yǐ bù qù	是 以 不 去

Admiring the most beautiful creates ugliness
Praising the greatest good creates evil

Existence and nonexistence arise together
Difficult and easy become each other
Long and short shape each other
High and low incline toward each other
Sound and tone harmonize each other
Before and after follow each other

Therefore the wise
    manage without controlling
    teach without telling
    tend to everything without favoritism
    raise without possessing
and claim no reward

Because they claim no reward
their rewards never diminish

All things possess features of the opposing yet complementary forces and characteristics of yin and yang. Neither is good, per se, nor bad. Neither is complete without the other. They are inseparable, interdependent, and interconnected. They are parts of a whole, representing its equally essential poles. *Existence and nonexistence arise together*. In the well-known yin-yang, or *taiji* (tai chi), symbol, the black yin and white yang teardrop shapes appear to chase each other around a circle in constant exchange of their position. Each shape contains a dot of its opposite color representing the seed of its inevitable change from one phase to the other. Between the two shapes is the sinuous Path that navigates its way perfectly between yin and yang, between darkness and light in the human psyche.

Yang represents the sunny side of the mountain, bright light, the strong, hard, higher, and active and the masculine. Yin represents the shady side of the mountain, dark, passivity, emptiness, cold, yielding, and low and the feminine.

A major feature of Daoism is its reverence for all things yin. This is not because yin is superior but because it is subtler than yang—but not less powerful, less aggressive perhaps but no less assertive. Key characteristics of yin are receptiveness and the ability to yield. The flower that attracts the bee is yin. Yin is the empty space that is vital for making a clay bowl useful. The soft is yin, but like soft water flowing it will eventually erode even the hardest rock. Yin-yang appears in many verses of the *Daodejing*.

A second important concept introduced in this verse, where it is suggested that "the wise manage without controlling, teach without telling, tend to everything without favoritism and claim no reward," is the concept of *wuwei*, doing without doing, doing not–doing, relinquishing control, which is one of the key concepts of the *Daodejing* and the primary subject of the next verse.

This chapter also introduces *shengren*, which has been translated various ways but most commonly rendered as "the wise man" or "the sage." Its usage often refers to particular wise men who were ancient, skilled followers of the Dao. The term is somewhat open to interpretation, however, and I choose to translate the term in a way that is more immediate and personal to the contemporary reader. I usually translate *shengren* as "the wise." This does not assign gender, which I think is beneficial, and it allows you to read *shengren* as anybody who attains wisdom or behaves wisely, including yourself. I acknowledge that this is probably a deviation from the original meaning, and I apologize for that.

VERSE 3. *WEI WUWEI*: DO NOT-DOING

Wuwei characters (traditional)

3　三

bù shàng xián shǐ mín bù zhēng	不尚贤使民不争
bù guì nán dé zhī huò shǐ mín bù wéi dào	不贵唯得之货使民不为盗
bù jiàn kě yù shǐ mín shīn bù luàn	不见可欲使民心不乱
shì yǐ shèng rén zhī zhì	是以圣人之治
xū qí xīn shí qí fù	虚其心实其腹
ruò qí zhì jiàng qí gǔ	弱其志强其骨
cháng shǐ mín wú zhī wú yù	常使民无知无欲
shǐ fū zhì zhě bù gǎn wéi yě	使夫智者不敢为也
wéi wú wéi zé wú bù zhì	为无为则无不治

Diminishing celebrity limits striving
Moderating wealth limits theft
Restraining desire limits yearning

Therefore the wise govern by
    emptying hearts and filling bellies
    weakening ideology and strengthening bones
    showing people how to live simply   satisfied
    preempting challenges from the treacherous

Practicing not-doing to maintain balance

The first three verses of the *Daodejing* introduce three of its most important themes: Dao in verse 1, yin-yang and *wuwei* in verse 2, and here, *wuwei* again. We can understand a good proportion of the teachings of Laozi with these three concepts and a fourth, De, which will follow soon.

Wuwei is translated, more or less (and there will be no surprise that it is impossible to pin the term down definitively), as no-do, or not-doing, and extends itself to various iterations of nonaction, not interfering, not fussing over things, resisting the urge to control things, or not meddling. My favorite interpretation may be "not-forcing," meaning to do things in the most natural or uninhibited way.

First of all, *wuwei* has enormous practical value. It's a call to resist micromanaging people. Hire someone good, train them, and then let them do their thing. It's also a call to quit meddling with things, especially those that are already finished. Leave it. It's done. Move on.

Wuwei is not a call to laziness and shows up repeatedly in the *Daodejing* to guide various aspects of skillful or thoughtful nonintervention. An additional use of *wuwei* is to depict action that is skilled, well directed, and well timed. Beautiful action. Effortless action. Practiced and perfected action. What Laozi describes resembles what we sometimes call "flow"—the way you perform when you are "in the zone."

Wuwei is advocated right at the end of this verse as a means of maintaining balance. Three vices are presented as threats to balance: celebrity, wealth, and desire, which is to say fame, fortune, and lust. How to maintain balance in the face of such iconic human failings? Well, a few practical tips are offered: You can keep people out of trouble and show them how to live a simple, honest, humble life, but what is the most important thing you can do? Nothing. Do not-doing. *Wei wuwei.*

Wuwei is powerful advice for environmentalists. How should we save energy? With a more efficient engine, a more efficient turbine? A more efficient go-slowing machine? How should we save resources? With better plastics, better fertilizers? A better do-lessing machine? Maybe, but the most important thing we can do is slow down and do less.

VERSE 4. WHAT IS THE DAO?

Dalvik, Iceland

4 四

dào chōng ér yòng zhī huò bù yíng　道 冲 而 用 之 或 不 盈

yuān xī sì wàn wù zhī zōng　渊 兮 似 万 物 之 宗

cuò qí ruì jiě qí fēn　挫 其 锐 解 其 纷

hé qí guāng tóng qí chén　和 其 光 同 其 尘

zhàn xī sì huò cún　湛 兮 似 或 存

wú bù zhī shéi zhī zǐ　吾 不 知 谁 之 子

xiàng dì zhī xiān　象 帝 之 先

The Dao is an empty vessel
    that cannot be drained
It is bottomless
    and the forebear of all

It can blunt the sharp
    untangle the knotted
    soften the glaring

It is like settled dust
    like a deep pool

I do not know whose child it is
It seems like the ancestor of god

One of the things that irks me about religion is the certainty so many religious folk express about things for which there can be no certainty. Nobody knows how the universe was formed or how life began, and to pretend to know is a lie. Science knows a fair bit about these things but refrains from overclaiming, and yet religions seem so certain. The religious appear to think that unknowable mysteries are their realm and that they have some special right, some spiritual authority, to make stuff up. Perhaps they feel safe in making these claims because they assume that their stories can never be disproven, and perhaps this explains the vehemence directed at people such as Galileo and Darwin who make them look silly from time to time.

Daoism is the name for both a philosophy, *daojia*, and a religion, Daojiao, and the *Daodejing* is the most important document of both. The proponents of Daojiao, the religion, claim to understand origins and to be able to achieve immortality. The proponents of *daojia*, the philosophy, make no such claims. In this verse and some that follow, Laozi casts around in wonder at life and at the universe and posits that everything is connected by a mysterious force called the Dao. He has questions, astonishment, and a deep sense of the vastness, depth, agelessness, and interconnectedness of things. He waxes lyrical and ascribes all manner of biological and physical features to the Dao, but it is important to note that he doesn't insist that he has all the answers.

The descriptions of the Dao that Laozi uses in this verse will show up again in the book. The Dao can *blunt the sharp, untangle the knotted*, and *soften the glaring*. In verse 56 he will claim that the wise can control their sharpness, untangle themselves, and resist glaring. The Dao is like *settled dust, like a deep pool*. In verse 15 he will ask the question (one of my favorite lines) *Who, by stillness can let the muddy water clear?* Water appears frequently in the *Daodejing* as an object of metaphor.

But does this verse give us an answer to the question "What is the Dao?" No, not really, and neither will the entirety of the *Daodejing*. Although *it seems like the ancestor of God*, Laozi does *not know whose child it is*. But it is a useful guide: a sort of personal treasure map on which X marks the spot where you should begin to dig. To paraphrase Wendell Berry, it may not be the only way to find the truth or the easiest. But it is one way.[9]

VERSE 5. NATURE
IS RUTHLESS

Lake Michigan from Ludington State Park

5　五

tiān dì bù rén yǐ wàn wù wéi chú gǒu　天地不仁以万物为刍狗

shèng rén bù rén yǐ bǎi xìng wéi chú gǒu　圣人不仁以百姓为刍狗

tiān dì zhī jiān qí yóu tuó yào hū　天地之间其犹橐龠乎

xū ér bù qū dòng ér yù chū　虚而不屈动而愈出

duō yán shù qióng bù rú shǒu zhōng　多言数穷不如守中

Nature is ruthless
It has no special love for any creature
The wise are ruthless
They treat all people equally

The space between heaven and earth
is a bellows
Empty and yet inexhaustible
The more it is pumped
the more it produces

Words are not inexhaustible
Say less and remain centered

There was something about the word "humane" that bothered me for a long time until I finally unraveled it in my own mind. It struck me that we tend to use this word in relation to behaviors that cause death or pain. Humane suggests the sort of thoughtful and kind behavior of which a nonhuman animal would be incapable, such as the kindness involved in putting down a sick animal. What actually separates humans from other animals, however, is not so much the kindness but rather the cruelties of which we are capable. We inflict cruelties that the rest of nature could never fathom.

Kindness and cruelty, of the human kind, require a conscience. They are things understood by human minds. Dying at the teeth and claws of a predator—ripped open and eaten alive—might be one of the most horrifying prospects the human mind can consider, but predators have no intent to cause suffering. Their behavior is entirely pragmatic. There are a few instances where predators appear to be toying with their food, such as cats with mice and orcas with seals, but these are rare behaviors.

Only conscious minds can experience true suffering, and only human minds, which can understand the suffering of others' minds, can choose to devise and execute torture.

This verse reminds us that nature is simply ruthless. It is not cruel, it does not torture, and it does not intend to cause suffering. The wise, similarly, treat all people ruthlessly, which is to say pragmatically. They can be kind without boosting their own ego. They can be assertive and decisive without cruelty.

And just as nature is ruthless, so too is it endless. These lines in the second stanza are some of the most wonderful words ever written on the possibilities of sustainability: *The space between heaven and earth is a bellows. . . . The more it is pumped the more it produces.* As one organism dies it is consumed by another. Life goes on, and the organism's matter and energy are passed forward to the next organism. Stars die, explode into clouds of matter, and are drawn back together to form new stars, and the cosmos goes on. The more activity you observe in the world, in the cosmos, the more there is to be seen. It is astonishing, then, given the self-replenishing nature of nature, that we are able to cause such damage. The Dao is inexhaustible, but we are overwhelming its powers of replenishment right now.

Nature may be inexhaustible, but as Laozi reminds us with a cheeky humor that punctuates the *Daodejing*, words are not inexhaustible. *Say less*, he begs, *and remain centered.*

VERSE 6. GAIA

Organoponico Vivero in Alamar, Cuba

6 六

gǔ shén bù sǐ 谷神不死

shì wèi xuán pìn 是谓玄牝

xuán pìn zhī mén 玄牝之门

shì wèi tiān dì gēn 是谓天地根

mián mián ruò cún 绵绵若存

yòng zhī bù qín 用之不勤

The valley spirit never dies
Call her the mysterious female
Hers is the gateway
that birthed heaven and earth

She endures forever   an endless thread
Tireless and abundant

The gateway of the female? Yikes, Lao: anatomical enough? *Hers is the gateway that birthed heaven and earth.* The power of the world, in Laozi's mind, comes in yin form rather than yang, the power of the gentle and yielding, of soft shade, of the feminine. The valley spirit that never dies is presumably a reference to the Dao itself, and so the Dao is the mysterious female, and she is tireless and abundant.

Laozi's description is reminiscent of the Greek goddess Gaia, or Ge, which makes me think of the Gaia hypothesis advanced by British scientist James Lovelock.[10]

Lovelock, who died in 2022 at age 103, was investigating the idea life on Mars when he came up with his famous Gaia hypothesis, which is an excellent representation of the Dao at the planetary level. How, he wondered, would one be able to tell, across the gulf of space, if there was life on a planet? Or to flip the question: How would aliens know, from space, that there was life on Earth? Lovelock's insight was that a planet that hosted life would appear alive itself. Thus, we should think of Earth not as a planet with life on it but as a living planet.

A nonliving rock orbiting the sun would be boring. As its orbit shifted it would warm up or cool down according to simple thermodynamics. If its star got hotter, it would warm up. When it moved farther away it would cool. As the sun gradually got hotter, the nonliving planet would heat up too. Its chemical makeup would remain rather static. Once a blob of rock, always a blob of rock. A nonliving planet would be terribly boring, as most planets are. But Earth is not boring, not even from space.

Earth doesn't warm or cool as it should, and its chemistry behaves strangely. Rocks are converted into seashells, and seashells are converted back into rocks. Soil, Earth's biochemical carpet, trades and blends the nonliving, the living, and the dead, the boundaries among which blur and dissipate. Earth's atmosphere, once devoid of oxygen, is now replete with the stuff—all of it created by organisms. Global atmospheric carbon dioxide, meanwhile, increases each northern winter and decreases each northern summer. Observant aliens would be able to watch Earth breathe.

And from where and what did life on Earth arise? Life on Earth arose from Earth. Awoken by the energy of its star, this planet, once devoid of life, evolved into a planet replete with life. Or rather, this planet, birthed, according to Laozi, by the valley spirit, the mysterious female, once nonliving, came alive.

VERSE 7. UNSELFISHNESS AND SELFLESSNESS

Birch trees, Lake Superior

七

tiān cháng dì jiǔ	天长地久
tiān dì suǒ yǐ néng cháng qiě jiǔ zhě	天地所以能长且久者
yǐ qí bù zì shēng	以其不自生
gù néng cháng shēng	故能长生
shì yǐ shèng rén hòu qí shēn ér shēn xiān	是以圣人后其身而身先
wài qí shēn ér shēn cún	外其身而身存
fēi yǐ qí wú sī xié	非以其无私邪
gù néng chéng qí sī	故能成其私

Heaven and earth are eternal
Since they do not cling to life
they cannot be claimed by death

The wise put themselves last
and yet advance
keep to the outside
and yet remain centered
and through selflessness

find themselves

The structure of this verse is common in the *Daodejing*. First, an observation of the natural world is made—in this case that heaven and earth cannot be killed because they don't cling to life. Second, the wise are compared against this observation in order to reveal a preferred human behavior—in this case that the wise are unselfish and yet succeed. Finally, a more profound statement draws the first two together—in this case that the wise are not only unselfish but also selfless. Their selflessness keeps them centered and gives them a deeper awareness of their fluid place in the world.

Unselfishness is simple. It is easily understood and is recognized universally as a human good. In the Bible, "And the first shall be last, and the last first" (Matthew 20:6). In the Quran, "We feed you only for the sake of Allah, seeking neither reward nor thanks from you" (sura Al-Insaan 76:8). Here, *The wise put themselves last and yet advance.*

Selflessness, or no-self, is a much more opaque concept and is a condition advocated in many philosophies and religions. Daoism, Buddhism, the Sufi branch of Islam, Hinduism, Stoicism, and other philosophies and religions provide forms of meditation that can guide one toward selflessness. Buddhism offers the most extensive guidance on attaining no-self (*annata*, in Pali; *anatman*, in Sanskrit). In Islam and Christianity, prayer has an analogous avowed function, although the idea of no-self is antithetical to the idea of the soul. (The soul is a "self" that lives on after death.)

Selflessness, no-self, can be understood intellectually with relative ease. Consider that the cells in your body are constantly dying and being replaced. There is nothing static or permanent about you: you are not a thing but instead are a flow. Consider the "you" that you were as a fetus, an infant, a child, and a youth and that you are now and that you will be at 102. Same "self?" Same "you?" And, are you really apart from the rest of the world at all? You are assembled from the elements lying around on the surface of the planet, and soon enough you will be redistributed back into the mix. The no-self can be understood intellectually with arguments such as these, but it is still not easily felt.

No specific method is required or guaranteed to reach a state of selflessness, but it is necessary to investigate the truth of existence. Selflessness is a felt state of oneness with the environment, the cosmos, and it is available to anyone willing to investigate their own minds.

VERSE 8. AS HUMBLE
AS WATER

Ohio River spring flood waters near Tell City, Indiana

8 八

shàng shàn ruò shuǐ	上 善 若 水
shuǐ shàn lì wàn wù ér bù zhēng	水 善 利 万 物 而 不 争
chǔ zhòng rén zhī suǒ ě	处 众 人 之 所 恶
gù jǐ yú dào	故 几 于 道
jū shàn dì	居 善 地
xīn shàn yuān yú shàn rén	心 善 渊 与 善 仁
yán shàn xìn	言 善 信
zhēng shàn zhì	正 善 治
shì shàn néng	事 善 能
dòng shàn shí	动 善 时
fū wéi bù zhēng	夫 唯 不 争
gù wú yóu	故 无 尤

The highest good is like water
Water benefits everything without fuss
It settles in the lowest places
This is how it shows us the Path

Live in connection with the earth
Love generously
Speak the truth
Govern peacefully and in search of order
Work expertly
Act in time

Avoid conflict and contention
and there will be no regrets

Water is one of Laozi's favorite vehicles of metaphor and is used here to create some of his simplest and most powerful images as points of comparison. Water benefits everything without fuss: it is the epitome of generosity. Water is the stuff of life, the universal solvent, the most abundant molecular component of living things. Alive, organisms are plump and pliant, hydrated. Dehydrated, they die, stiff and shriveled (see v. 76). Water moves into the living, animates them, leaves them at death, and moves onward to animate another. Water illustrates the eternal Dao, the grand motivating force of the cosmos, and as it flows, creating streams, pools, rivers, and oceans, it shows us how to shape a path.

Water *settles in the lowest places*, which is to say the most low-down, loathsome places: its nature is to seek out these places. Water is the epitome of humility, and it *shows us the Path*, the Way. Imagine a molecule of water falling on the Tibetan Plateau. Watch it as it moves downward, joins rivulets and streams and rivers, cascades off the mountains, pounds its way through steep valleys past towns and through cities, pours into the flatlands, oozes across rice paddies, and seeps into mangrove swamps and out into the deep ocean, where it sinks down into the unfathomable depths. Water's natural state is to flow downward, to be the reliable fundament of life on Earth.

Hence the life advice given in this verse: Be simple, honest, humble. Be effective and timely in your actions. *Avoid conflict and contention and there will be no regrets.* Be like water. Laozi advises us to recognize that we are not above or outside nature, not apart from nature, but instead are a part of it. *Live in connection with the earth*, he advises—like water. Living in connection with nature, mirroring its peacefulness and working expertly and in time, will tend to guide us away from strife and into a more natural flow. To follow the Dao is to be natural and follow the ways and rhythms of nature—and in nature there are few better teachers than water.

And a passing thought: What would Laozi think about the way our culture has treated water? The way we have drained aquifers and dried up lakes and rivers. The algal blooms from the leaching of nitrogen fertilizers, cyanobacterial blooms from wasted phosphorous. Salinized land from excessive irrigation. The death of the Aral Sea. Industrial effluent. Sewage. Ocean gyres circulating as vast islands of plastic...

VERSE 9. MODERATION

Candle

9 九

chí ér yíng zhī bù rú qí jǐ 持而盈之不如其已

chuǎi ér ruì zhī bù kě cháng bǎo 揣而锐之不可长保

jīn yù mǎn táng mò zhī néng shǒu 金玉满两锐之能守

fù guì ér jiāo zì yí qí jiù 富贵而骄自遗其咎

gōng suì shēn tuì 功遂身退

tiān zhī dào 天之道

Overfill a bowl and it will spill
Oversharpen a blade and its edge will brittle
Hoard wealth and your home will be a target for thieves
Amass prestige and you invite downfall and disgrace

Do good work and then step back
This is the Way of heaven

Moderation is the theme of a number of verses in the *Daodejing*. Here, the advice is given simply and plainly. Do good work and then step back. The advice appears to be written as personal advice, but I also see it as advice to today's culture. With over eight billion of us to be fed, how dare the wealthy overfill their bowls? Likewise, when we oversharpen our blades and hoard wealth, we invite collective *downfall and disgrace*.

The call here is not for a complete renunciation but instead for balance. Go ahead and take some soup from the bowl, but don't be greedy. Yes, sharpen the blade, that's fine, and live in a comfortable home. You're not expected to live like a pauper, just don't be greedy. Don't take more than a reasonable share.

The fourth line of this verse is particularly interesting. Moderation is advised not just to avoid spilled bowls, brittle blades, and becoming a target for thieves but also to avoid becoming a target for one's own ego. *Amass prestige and you invite downfall and disgrace*. Prestige does not need to be sought, and gaining it can make you protective of it. Living in moderation doesn't mean being moderate only in your collection of material knickknacks but also in your collection of egoic knickknacks. People seek prestige in many ways. We are desperate to be seen as successful, competent, and virtuous. Our tendency to seek prestige and to make ostentatious displays of having attained it with ornate houses, fast cars, shiny jewelry, and fancy clothes costs the environment dearly.

As Welsh author Alwyn Rhys commented, "We cannot escape by forging on, resolutely and regardless, driven by the unmitigated inertia of outworn habits, until we have forced ourselves over the brink in the 'giant step for mankind' nobody needs. When you have reached the edge of an abyss, the only progressive move you can make is to step backward."[11]

Can the ethics prescribed in the *Daodejing* bring people to moderate their behavior in a ravenous culture that is already spilling over the edge of the abyss? Yes, it can, and I think it must have done exactly that for thousands of people over the millennia. But can it affect enough people to deflect the tragic path our civilization faces? Probably not. Its advice has been readily available for over two thousand years, and it has been more often ignored than heeded. There's no obvious reason to expect that to change in the twenty-first century.

VERSE 10. MEDITATION

Zen (Chan) meditation

10　　十

zǎi yíng pò bào yī néng wú lí hū　　载 营 魄 抱 一 能 无 离 于

zhuān qì zhì róu néng rú yīng ér hū　　专 气 致 柔 能 如 婴 儿 于

dí chú xuán lǎn néng wú cī hū　　涤 除 玄 览 能 无 疵 于

ài gúo zhì mín néng wú wéi hū　　爱 国 治 民 能 无 为 于

tiān mén kāi gé néng wéi cí hū　　天 门 开 阖 能 为 雌 于

míng bái sì dá néng wú zhī hū　　明 白 四 达 能 无 知 乎

shēng zhī chù zhī shēng ér bù yǒu　　生 之 畜 之 生 而 不 有

wéi ér bù shì　　为 而 不 恃

zhǎng ér bù zǎi　　长 而 不 宰

shè wèi xuán dé　　是 谓 玄 德

Can you unify the elements of your soul
    and keep them from dividing?
Can you focus your vital breath
    until you are as supple as a newborn?
Can you polish your inner mirror
    until its reflection is pure?
Can you love people and guide them
    without manipulation?

Though the gates of heaven may open and close
    can you abide like a bird with her nestlings?
Though your mind may penetrate the secrets of the cosmos
    can you continue to practice nonaction?

To give birth and nurture
To bear without possessing
To act without claiming
To lead without dominating
This is profound virtue

The ancient Eastern philosophies and religions—Daoism, Confucianism, Hinduism, and Buddhism—exchanged various ideas and practices as they coevolved. One thread that they have in common is the mind-training practice of meditation, which probably had independent origins in China (Daosim, as shown by its appearance here in the *Daodejing* and elsewhere) and India (Hinduism) but reached its pinnacle in Buddhism following the great insights of Siddhartha Gotama, who became the Buddha. The benefits of meditation can be accessed without any need to be involved in any of the religions traditionally associated with the practice, which is how Laozi and the Buddha would presumably have preferred things. The fundamental insights and benefits of meditation are laid out here by Laozi.

The first stanza speaks of the improvement of the mind through meditation. The uninvestigated mind appears as some "self" or "me" that is randomly tangled up in all manner of thoughts of genius or folly. Can you study it to better understand and unify your own consciousness? Focusing on the breath (here extended to the larger concept of the vital breath, the Qi) is a common practice of mindfulness meditation, which can help control unskillful trains of thought. The breath serves as a bodily "anchor" to which you can return your focus should your thoughts drift. The *inner mirror*, can you polish it? Can you look at yourself clearly and yet nonjudgmentally? Can you *love* and *guide* people *without manipulation*? These are some of the core ideas of meditation.

Windows and mirrors are useful mental objects of mindfulness and meditation. Enlightenment can be imagined through the metaphor of the window-mirror. One moment all you see is yourself, mirrored in the glass, then suddenly the mirror becomes a window, and you see through to the other side. You have seen behind the curtain: a sudden enlightenment.

The second stanza digs deeper into wrestling the mind under control. Can you train the mind to minimize negative thoughts and stop it from tormenting you? Can you find selflessness? Can you accept yourself as a true and honest part of the great, flowing Path of existence, the Dao, of which you are a beautiful but transient part? And, having gained greater insight and wisdom, can you resist the urge to lord it over everyone? *Can you continue to practice nonaction?*

The third stanza gives advice on what to do with your meditation-trained mind. This is not complicated. Tread lightly. Don't be possessive. Be happy. Be kind. Is all.

VERSE 11. THE SILENCE
BETWEEN NOTES

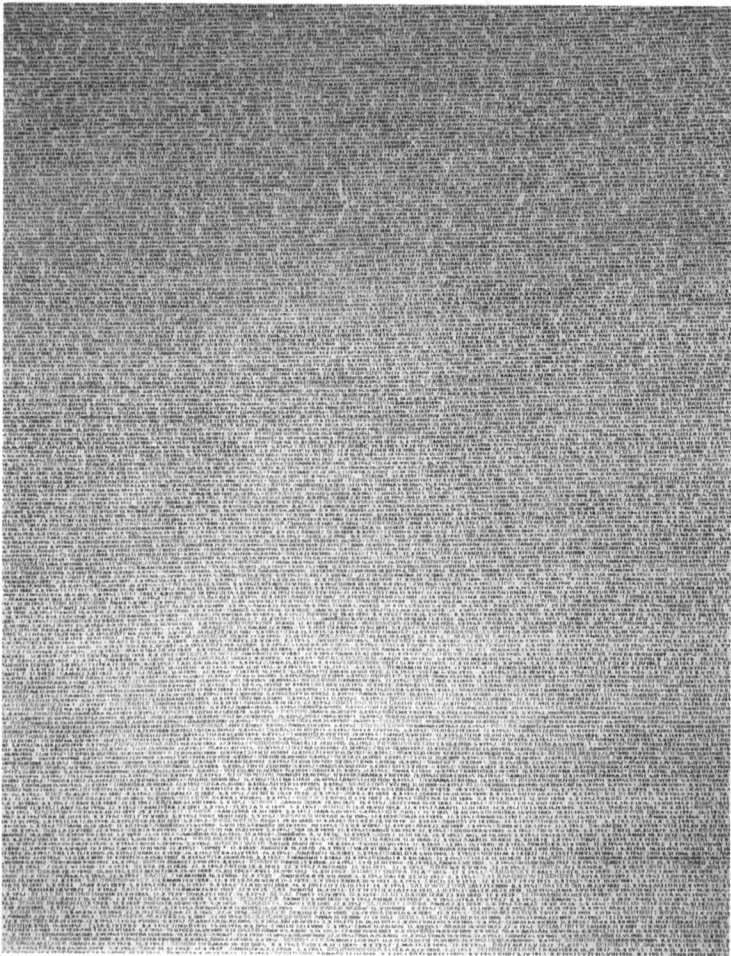

Names of Holocaust victims on the walls of the Pinkas Synagogue
at the Old Jewish Cemetery, Prague, Czechia

11 十一

sān shí fú gòng yī gū	三 十 幅 共 一 毂
dāng qí wú yǒu chē zhī yòng	当 其 无 有 车 之 用
shān zhé yǐ wéi qì	埏 埴 以 为 器
dāng qí wú yǒu qì zhī yòng	当 其 无 有 器 之 用
záo hù yǒu yǐ wéi shì	凿 户 牖 以 为 室
dāng qí wú yǒu shì zhī yòng	当 其 无 有 室 之 用
gù yǒu zhī yǐ wéi lì	故 有 之 以 为 利
wú zhī yǐ wéi yòng	无 之 以 为 用

Thirty spokes join at the hub
but the axle turns in its empty space

Clay is shaped to make a bowl
but its hollow is what you use

Doors and windows are cut to make a house
creating the voids that allow you to enter and live

What is present makes a thing valuable
What is absent makes it work

My sons and I love the movie *Cloud Atlas* in which one of Ben Whishaw's characters, Robert Frobisher, uses the line "like the silence between notes that holds to key to all music." I love that line, which comes from Claude Debussy, who said, "La musique est le silence entre les notes." His music can be decidedly spare. You can hear his genius as a weaving together of music and silence. As two examples, I suggest listening to the famous piano pieces *Clair de Lune* and *La Fille aux Cheveux de Lin.* If you get a chance to hear Daniel Hallett play one of these on the marimba, you have been blessed. Both are weirdly beautiful, with expressive silences. Another stunning example is Gustav Mahler's sixth song, "Der Abschied" (The Farwell), in his remarkable *Das Lied von der Erde* (The Song of the Earth). The haunting music, written as Mahler grieved after the death of his daughter, wends sparsely around a sequence of tender Tang dynasty poems. With *Das Lied von der Erde*, the master of the giant, bombastic symphony created a masterpiece of musical emptiness, musical *wuwei*.

The notes are yang, and the silence between them is yin. Laozi would approve. In this verse, the wooden spokes are yang, while the empty space in which the axle turns is yin—and just as important. Likewise, the yang clay of the bowl forms a yin space where food and drink are held; the yang bricks and mortar of a house support the yin spaces through which you move. You cannot own or sell the silence between notes, the hollow in a wheel, a bowl, or a window opening, but the voids are the necessary spaces that make their objects function. The note and the silence are equally important. They complete each other. They are yin and yang: inseparable and interdependent parts of a whole.

A central idea of Buddhist meditation is to achieve a state of perfect emptiness known as sunyata, a form of selflessness that brings deep awareness. I'm not sure exactly what practitioners mean by sunyata, having not experienced it, but a quiet yin state of mind is a lovely place to be: the silence between thoughts.

This verse also reveals a fascinating link between Daoism and Buddhism. The central theme of Buddhism is to understand the appearance and eradication of *dukkha*, which is translated (clunkily) into English as "suffering," "craving," "dissatisfaction," or something similar. In Pali, however, the first language into which the orations of the Buddha were transcribed, one understanding of *dukkha* is "when the axle fits poorly in the wheel hub."

VERSE 12. RESTRAIN THE SENSES

Clouds over the Atlantic

12　十二

wǔ sè lìng rén mù máng	五色令人目盲
wǔ yīn lìng rén ěr lóng	五音令人耳聋
wǔ wèi lìng rén kǒu shuǎng	五味令人口爽
chí chéng tián liè lìng rén xīn fā kuáng	驰骋畋猎令人心发狂
nán dé zhī huò lìng rén xíng fáng	难得之货令人行妨
shì yǐ shèng rén wéi fù bù wéi mù	是以圣人为腹不为目
gù qù bǐ qǔ cǐ	故去彼取此

The five colors blind the eye
The five notes deafen the ear
The fives tastes dull the palate

Aggressions   chasing hunting   derange the mind
Ambitions   power riches   lead one astray

The wise tend to the belly not the eyes

They reject that
They accept this

The five colors are red, green, yellow, black, and white. The five notes are G, A, B, D, and E. The five tastes are sweet, salt, sour, bitter, and umami. We desire fine entertainments. We crave rich foods. We pursue excitements such as hunting and have ambitions for wealth and power.

All these things are the surface desires introduced in verse 1. They are integral to our experience of the world, and experiencing the world fully is a good thing, but the joys of the senses are experiences of the outer world, and they must be recognized as such. Experiencing them is healthy, but craving them can tie our inner world in knots. Life's pleasures can be deeply rewarding, but chasing them can lead us astray, especially when reaching one goal merely leads us to crave the next. Life can be spent chasing elusive, magical goals without ever fully noticing any of them: "When I have X I will be happy," we tell ourselves, but will we? So many goals—a faster car, a bigger house—are fools' errands.

Craving sense pleasures can lead to dependency and addiction. Addiction may come from the use of chemicals such as nicotine and cocaine that induce specific physiological reactions when they bind to neuroreceptors in the brain, but it can equally be behavioral, such as an addiction to gambling. There are similarities among all forms of dependency and addiction, linked to the release of dopamine in the brain as a neurochemical reward. Although they knew little of the physiological or biochemical mechanisms of addiction, the earliest schools of Buddhism and Daoism had a solid practical grasp of this. Unrecognized cravings and unrestrained desires *lead us astray* and *derange the mind*. Constant striving is a form of chronic, low-level madness.

The wise, says Laozi, *tend to the belly, not the eyes*. They respond to reasonable desires such as the belly's need for sustenance but resist outward and excessive desires and craving that might be sought by the eyes. They learn to live simply and yet experience what they have more richly and fully, without wishing for more. The core of this practice is mindfulness, which has the power to limit both the perils of addiction and the mundane, quotidian sufferings caused by endless craving.

And finally, Laozi simply says, *They reject that. They accept this.* He often ends with these enigmatic little statements. I imagine Laozi holding his hands out, palms up, with a wry smile and a little shrug.

VERSE 13. THE MIND
IS ITS OWN PLACE

Addis Ababa, Ethiopia

13 十三

chǒng rǔ ruò jīng	宠辱若惊
guì dà huàn ruò shēn	贵大患若身
hé wèi chǒng rǔ ruò jīng	何谓宠辱若惊
chǒng wéi xià	宠为下
dé zhī ruò jīng	得之若惊
shī zhī ruò jīng	失之若惊
shì wèi chǒng rǔ ruò jīng	是谓宠辱若惊
hé wèi guì dà huàn ruò shēn	何谓贵大患若身
wú suǒ yǐ yǒu dà huàn zhě wéi wú yǒu shēn	吾所以有大患者为吾有身
jí wú wú shēn wú yǒu hé huàn	及吾无身吾有何患
gù guì yǐ shēn wéi tiān xià	故贵以身为天下
ruò kě jì tiān xià	若可寄天下
ài yǐ shēn wéi tiān xià	爱以身为天下
ruò kě tuō tiān xià	若可托天下

Be equally wary of honor and disgrace

Regard mental anguish as physical pain

Why do we say
Be equally wary of honor and disgrace?
Honor can demoralize
We are apprehensive about gaining it
We fear the disgrace of losing it

Why do we say
Regard mental anguish as physical pain?
The mind devises its own suffering
but without a physical self
how can it be conscious of suffering?

The person who tends to their self
can be trusted to lead people
and care for the world

This verse continues the theme of the last by examining the statement *regard mental anguish as physical pain*, which is reminiscent of the famous line from John Donne's *Paradise Lost*: "The mind is its own place, and in itself it can make a heaven of hell, a hell of heaven." The verse also reminds me of Yoda, from *Star Wars*: "Fear leads to anger. Anger leads to hate. Hate leads to suffering." The Jedi are decidedly Daoist (with an admixture of Buddhist and Stoic), and Yoda is basically a short, green Laozi. The Force is surely George Lucas's manifestation of the Dao.[12]

Physical pain is acutely felt and easily understood. It is immediate and obvious, and we know it well and in many forms. Mental pain, meanwhile, is much more puzzling and mysterious. We understand it very poorly and often don't even recognize it when it strikes. Perhaps this should not be surprising, since all pain, physical or mental, is processed and interpreted by the mind. Why would the mind conclude that it is the cause of your suffering? And yet, we know that physical and mental pain are intimately linked. Stress gives us a stiff neck. Fear makes us sick to the stomach. Anxiety is exhausting. Laozi exhorts us to recognize the vulnerabilities of the mind and to pay attention to our mental health.

A useful discourse on this subject is offered by the Buddha's concept of the second dart, which represents our tendency to react to pain, misfortune, or injustice—unavoidable "first darts"—with damaging mental reactions such as anger and hatred. We fire these unnecessary second darts at ourselves. Anger is a classic second dart. Something may have happened to cause us pain, but the statement "you made me angry" is never true. You may have caused me pain, but in regard to the anger that followed, I allowed my own mind to cause that.

Laozi also tells us *be equally wary of honor and disgrace*, a warning about the mental suffering brought on by craving the esteem of others. We have a deep-seated desire for other people to think well of us, to have them deem us honorable. We project ourselves into their minds and evaluate their evaluation of us. This is nuts and convoluted, but our minds are making these complex "How am I perceived?" calculations all the time. What people think of us is one of our greatest preoccupations. To believe that you are viewed badly is to suffer disgrace. But do people actually think that, or is it just your brain chattering? We tie ourselves in unnecessary knots and cause ourselves unnecessary mental pain by seeking honor in the unknowable minds of others, so disgrace is never more than a thought away. It is better perhaps to live simply and honestly and resist the mind's penchant for craving honor.

VERSE 14. THE
GREAT MYSTERY

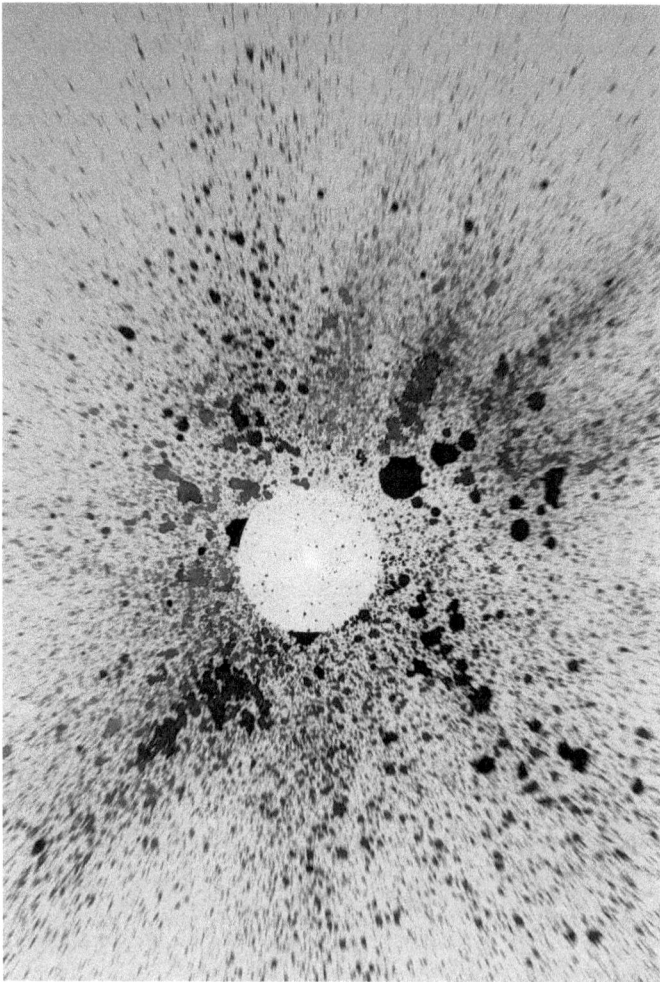

Cosmic splatter

14　　十四

shì zhī bù jiàn míng yuē yí　视 之 不 见 名 曰 夷

tīng zhī bù wén míng yuē xī　听 之 不 闻 名 曰 希

bó zhī bù dé míng yuē wēi　搏 之 不 得 名 曰 微

cǐ sān zhě bù kě zhì jié gù hún ér wéi yī　此 三 者 不 可 致 诘 故 混 而 为 一

qí shàng bù jiǎo qí xià bù mèi　其 上 不 皦 其 下 不 昧

shéng shéng bù kě míng fù guī yú wú wù　绳 绳 不 可 名 复 归 于 无 物

shì wèi wú zhuàng zhī zhuàng wú wù zhī xiàng　是 谓 无 状 之 状 无 物 之 象

shì wèi hū huǎng　是 谓 惚 恍

yíng zhī bù jiàn qí shǒu　迎 之 不 见 其 首

suí zhī bù jiàn qí hòu　随 之 不 见 其 后

zhí gǔ zhī dào yǐ yù jīn zhī yǒu　执 古 之 道 以 御 今 之 有

néng zhī gǔ shǐ shì wèi dào jì　能 知 古 始 是 谓 道 纪

Look for it   it can't be seen
Listen for it   it can't be heard
Reach for it   it can't be touched
These three mysteries merge as one

In rising it does not brighten
In setting it does not darken
An unbroken thread of nameless things
from now back to the chaos
before the first

Call it the formless form
the imageless image
the unthought thought

Face it and you see no beginning
Follow it and you see no end

Hold tight to the Ancient Way
in order to master the present
To know the ancient beginnings
is the essence of the Dao

In Douglas Adams's *The Hitchhiker's Guide to the Galaxy*, the answer is forty-two.[13] To the world's religions, it is some version of God or gods (or Flying Spaghetti Monsters). To physicists, it is some combination of matter and energy, with its origins, well, its latest origins at least, in the Big Bang. To Laozi, it is some unknown and unknowable cosmic force.

Just how the universe "works" is, of course, a great mystery, or a complicated hodgepodge of knowns and unknowns. And perhaps it doesn't need to be understood, but the human mind seems to have this desire to give the universe form, to personify it, and to endow it with motives. Laozi is not immune to this desire, but his approach is somewhat unique in the way it resists dogmatic claims. I imagine him looking up at the sky at night, reaching out for the animating force of the cosmos. He can feel it, somehow, elusively, indescribably, something swirling around, but it *can't be seen, can't be heard, can't be touched.*

This verse is Laozi's third attempt to describe the Dao. It is a beautiful verse, intoxicated with the mystery of things. The Dao is everywhere and nowhere, all-powerful and nonexistent. I am particularly taken with the *unbroken thread of nameless things from now back to the chaos before the first,* which suggests that Laozi had a deep sense of the flow of life evolving from simplicity to complexity as a continuum. The Dao is Laozi's sense of the deep connectedness of things.

Charles Darwin wouldn't come along for more than two millennia and a continent away, but Darwin wasn't the first person to have a sense of the evolutionary flow of life on Earth. He was the first to give it detail, description, and a firm, logical basis. Ralph Waldo Emerson sensed it before that in his essay *Nature* (1836). Lucretius (99–50 BCE) hinted at it in *On the Nature of Things.* Lord Krishna explained it to Arjuna on the eve of the Great Battle described in the Bhagavad Gita: "Know that through lucid knowledge one sees in all creatures a single, unchanging existence, undivided." Laozi sensed that *to know the ancient beginnings is the essence of Dao.*

And the Dao is also a path that can be followed: *Hold tight to the Ancient Way in order to master the present.* Laozi had a great reverence for the complicated nature of things and a deep sense that the virtues he advocates: modesty, moderation, compassion, honesty, and humility are best attained by observing the workings of the cosmos and following the path of its teachings.

VERSE 15. THE ANCIENTS
OF THE ANCIENTS

The White House (Kinii' Ni Gai), an ancient ruin of the Hisatsinom. Canyon de Chelly, Arizona

15 十五

gǔ zhī shàn wéi shì zhě wēi miào
古之善为士者微妙

xuán tōng shēn bù kě shí
玄通深不可识

fū wéi bù kě shí gù jiàng wéi zhī róng
夫唯不可识故强为之容

yù xī ruò dōng shè chuān
豫兮若冬涉涉川

yóu xī ruò wèi sì lín
犹兮若畏四邻

yǎn xī qí ruò róng
俨兮其若客

huàn xī ruò bīng zhī jiāng shì
涣兮若冰之将释

dūn xī qí ruò pǔ
敦兮其若朴

kuàng xī qí ruò gǔ
旷兮其若谷

hún xī qí ruò zhuó
混兮其若浊

dàn xī qí ruò hǎi
澹兮其若海

liáo xī ruò wú zhǐ
飂兮若无止

shú néng zhuó yǐ jìng zhī xú qīng
孰能浊以静之徐清

shú néng ān yǐ dòng zhī xú shēng
孰能安以动之徐生

bǎo cǐ dào zhě bù yù yíng
保此道者不欲盈

fū wéi bù yíng gù néng bì ér xīn chéng
唯不盈故能蔽而新成

The ancient masters were subtle
   Mysterious   penetrating   profound
   too profound to understand
but perhaps we can describe them

Cautious as if crossing a frozen river
Vigilant as if sensing enemies on all four sides
Courteous like polite house guests
Yielding like melting ice
Sincere and uncomplicated like the uncarved block
Receptive like a valley
   Opaque   inscrutable   like muddy water

Who by nothing but stillness
   can render muddy water clear?
Who by persistent gentleness
   can quicken the moribund?

Those who follow the Path guard against excess
and are beyond the concerns
of old age and decrepitude

Two thousand five hundred years ago Laozi, an ancient to us, spoke of his own ancients. It seems that we always revere the strange, unknowable, vaguely remembered sages of the distant past. Did Laozi's ancients revere their own ancients? And them theirs? Or, here's a thought: perhaps some stories of the ancients reach back into yet deeper times, earlier truths, and more ancient tales.

In the story of Cain and Abel in Genesis, for example, who were those feuding brothers? Not brothers but rather place markers for a clash between an ancient nomadic herder culture and an emerging agrarian culture in the Middle East. The Cain kills Abel story represents the displacement of herders by farmers, indigenous land stewards by colonizers. And what about the even older *Epic of Gilgamesh*, which was etched onto clay tablets in Cuneiform nearly four thousand years ago? Well, the travails of Enkidu, Shamhat, and Gilgamesh quite likely gave rise to much of the Garden of Eden and Noah's flood stories, ancient stories with their origins in yet more ancient times. Could the flood stories, for example, have their origins in the collapse of ice dams at the end of the last ice age, over ten thousand years ago?

It is far from clear, but some of the *Daodejing* may have very early preagrarian origins. Discussions of power invoke a sense of encroachment into hunted-and-gathered environments by organized farming cultures. The soft power of the female is frequently contrasted with the direct power of the male, which we normally interpret as a direct exploration of yin-yang contrasts but may suggest older Paleolithic origins. Some of this text may have its origins in oral traditions that existed long before the first characters were set down in seal script. So, Laozi describes *his* ancients as the ultimate masters of the Dao. These are not vainglorious colonizers despoiling their way across the landscape. They are cautious, vigilant, courteous, yielding, sincere, receptive, and inscrutable.

One of my favorite lines comes from this verse: *Who, by nothing but stillness, can render muddy water clear?* This is a wonderful image of the ultimate *wuwei*. What technology would we use today? Filtration? Reverse osmosis? Centrifugation? The ancients would simply be still. Wait. Let the muddy water settle. And what might you see when the water clears? You might see through the pool, to the bottom. You might see a reflection of the sky. You might even see yourself. You might see no-self. Slow down and let the muddy water of the mind settle. Become tranquil. Find clarity.

VERSE 16. RETURN TO THE ROOT

Poppies

16　十六

zhì xū jí shǒu jìng dǔ	致虚极守静笃
wàn wù bìng zuò wú yǐ guān fù	万物并作吾以观复
fū wù yún yún gè fù guī qí gēn	夫物芸芸各复归其根
guī gēn yuē jìng shì wèi fù mìng	归根曰静是谓复命
fù mìng yuē cháng zhī cháng yuē míng	复命曰常知常曰明
bù zhī cháng wàng zuò xiōng	不知常妄作凶
zhī cháng róng róng nǎi gōng	知常容容乃公
gōng nǎi quán quán nǎi tiān	公乃全全乃天
tiān nǎi dào	天乃道
dào nǎi jiǔ méi shēn bù dài	道乃久没身不殆

Attain complete emptiness
Maintain absolute stillness

All living things arise in unison
   and their arising is a return
A flower grows
   blooms
     returns to the root

Returning to the root is peaceful
   a return to one's original nature
   to the immutable
Knowing this is true wisdom
Not knowing this is disastrous

To know what endures is to be
enlightened   majestic   heavenly
in accordance with the Eternal Path

Following the Path leads to immortality
Though the self is ephemeral
there is no fear

The simplest image to conjure is that of a daffodil or a tulip, its bulb breaking in the spring as the days lengthen, the plant's internal clock (a phytochrome pigment system) detecting the approaching equinox, a long period of cold having degraded dormancy-enforcing metabolites, and spring has come. It is raining. A cascade of hydrolytic enzymes is activated, and the shoot explodes from the top of the bulb and surges from the ground. Fibrous roots scurry down into the wet soil. The plant comes to life. But it was never dead, of course. It will grow, send up a flowering shoot, and unveil a profligate display of absurdly ostentatious flowers. The flowers will shine and then fade, wilt, and abscise. The leaves will yellow, brown, and collapse. The plant will return to the root, not dead, of course, simply as part of its life cycle, a part neither more or less remarkable than any other.

This is how all things are, possessing neither beginnings nor endings, including humans. As Alan Watts said, "We are not born to the world but of it, and so to it, we must return," and "the world peoples in rather the same way an apple tree apples."[14] *Knowing this is true wisdom. Not knowing this is disastrous.*

Ecologists have an intellectual understanding of one of the key tenets of the Dao because they have learned to see nature not as a collection of things but instead as a system or, more accurately, as a system of systems. To contemplate the Dao is to take a journey beyond even this systems-within-systems vision and into deep ecology. Not only do you begin to see both the forest and the trees, but you also see what the trees were and will be and what the forest was and will become. The leaves die a million deaths, but the tree goes on. The trees die a million deaths, but the forest goes on. *Though the self is ephemeral there is no fear.* The forest burns to the ground. This is just a phase: it grows back. An ice age forces it to move south. The forest dances across the landscape and then returns as the ice recedes. Perhaps the forest will eventually be destroyed, but its pieces will be distributed into whatever follows, just as the trees were once ferns, the ferns were once algae, and everything alive was once the crust of a young, lifeless planet.

This, claims Laozi, is immortality. You repeatedly emerge from natures in this form or that and return. You repeatedly emerge from the cosmos is this form or that and return. How long before you find yourself in a different star?

VERSE 17. UNOBTRUSIVE LEADERSHIP

Hoophouse build, Purdue Student Farm, West Lafayette, Indiana

17　十七

tài shàng xià zhī yǒu zhī　太上下知有之

qí cì qīn ér yù zhī　其次亲而誉之

qí cì wèi zhī　其次畏之

qí cì wǔ zhī　其次侮之

xìn bù zú yān yǒu bù xìn yān　信不足焉有不信焉

yōu xī qí guì yán　悠令其贵言

gōng chéng shì suì　功成事遂

bǎi xìng jiē wèi wǒ zì rán　百姓皆谓我自然

Great leaders are barely known
Next are the leaders people admire
Next are the leaders people fear
Worst are the leaders people despise

If you give no trust
you will receive no trust

When the humble leader has done her work
the people will say
"Look! We did it all ourselves!"

This is the first of a number of verses about leadership in which the common thread is *wuwei*. Lead without being a control freak, without micromanaging, by resisting the urge to be a helicopter mom (or dad), being mindful of *wuwei*'s varied wisdoms of non-action, not forcing, not meddling. This particular verse is also linked with the next two verses in speaking about simplicity and humility.

The two worst kinds of leaders are the feared and the despised, and it is revealed that of the two, Laozi prefers the feared. During the Zhou dynasty, especially the aptly named Warring States period, people would have had ample opportunity to experience the problems caused by bad leaders. Some of these leaders would have been feared because they were brutal or heavy-handed, and such leadership is worthy of little praise, but Laozi prefers it to incompetence. There is a suggestion of conservatism in Laozi's politics here, and the sentiment is reminiscent of Thomas Hobbes's *Leviathan*, which argues for a government always powerful enough to be in control. Nothing is worse than a government so incompetent that it is despised. Social disintegration is threatened when the people lose respect for their leaders. To Laozi, even a brutal leader is better than anarchy.

So, there's a warning: the worst leader is the incompetent one, and even a despot is better. Job one of government is to govern. Given this minimum requirement, however, Laozi advocates for humble, modest leadership. A leader who is admired is a wonderful thing, but even better is a competent leader who quietly motivates people to be the best versions of themselves. How many leaders are satisfied with a great result and feel no need to take the credit?

This is the face-value reading of this verse, but I sense that there might be more here. There's anarchy, in the colloquial sense, which implies madness and mayhem, but there's also anarchy, in the Petr Kropotkin sense, which implies a profoundly egalitarian society. I tend to think of Laozi as comfortable with hierarchy, but the phrase *Look! We did it all ourselves!* is pretty powerful stuff.

The final line of this verse is a difficult and fascinating translation. *Wo ziran* translates more literally as "we naturally" or "we nature," and *ziran*—nature, naturally—is derived from combining *zi*, meaning "self," and *ran*, meaning "so," "right," or "correct." Thus, *ziran* also means something like "self-so" or "as-it-is-ness." The combination of the naturalness of *ziran* with the effortlessness of *wuwei* provides a basic template for living in harmony with the Dao.

VERSE 18. FALSE LOYALTY

Asbury Church and Cemetery, Asbury, Illinois

18 十八

dà dào fèi yǒu rén yì	大道废有仁义
huì zhì chū yǒu dà wěi	慧智出有大伪
liù qīn bù hé yǒu xiào cí	六亲不和有孝慈
guó jiā hūn luàn yǒu zhōng chén	国家昏乱有忠臣

When the great Path is deserted
humanity and morality take its place

When cleverness and intellect dominate
hypocrisy soon follows

When the family falls into conflict
we hear talk of dutiful sons

When the country falls into chaos
the patriots present themselves

Patriots are a very bad sign, particularly those self-proclaimed flag-waving, fist-thumping, nationalistic patriots. I'm picturing the US Capitol in 2021 and the German Reichstag in 1933. I'm remembering all the times I've had to sit through a dreary National Anthem before getting to watch a game. And dutiful sons? Ugh. What a ghastly idea. The day my boys say "Yes, father" to me without irony will be the day I know I have failed as a parent.

A little less clear is Laozi's warning against cleverness and intellect. A careless reading of the *Daodejing* might give us the impression that Laozi is anti-intellectual. He is not, but he does warn us against arrogant and hypocritical intellectual superiority and grandiosity, which he sees as barriers to enlightenment. The Dao shows the way, and an honest, open mind will follow it more easily than a conniving, calculating mind that seeks its own studied self-interest. There is no negotiating with honesty, humility, and openness. If you're arguing with the path, you're not on it.

Another word that might be used here instead of cleverness is craftiness. Laozi is thinking about a particular sort of cleverness that is manipulative or devious. This idea pops up again in the next verse and in verse 65. My impression is that Laozi is comfortable with intelligence and knowledge but wants to remind us that these abilities can be applied selfishly as well as attentively and are not the same thing as wisdom.

Working backward through the verse, this brings us to the first couplet where Laozi criticizes humanity and morality. They're better than cleverness, intellect, duty, and patriotism, but they fall short of the highest ideal, which is to trust yourself to follow the wide open Path with honesty and humility.

This, I think, is a wonderful insight. Morals are cultural shortcuts that lead us toward polite, acceptable, mannerly behavior, but if our cultural group is off the rails, thanks to misguided duty and patriotism (storming the US Capitol in 2021 and the Reichstag in 1933 perhaps), we must have the strength of character to find the compassionate path irrespective of our cultures mores and morals.

A life without false morals, despite the absence of easy-to-follow social rules, is the ultimate reward. When we learn to navigate the world with freedom and honesty, trusting our own balance and with the liberty to make our own decisions, life is wide and huge and full.

VERSE 19. THE UNCARVED BLOCK

Bamboo

19　十九

jué shèng qì zhì　绝 圣 弃 智

mín lì bǎi bèi　民 利 百 倍

jué rén qì yì　绝 仁 弃 义

mín fù xiào cí　民 复 孝 慈

jué qiǎo qì lì　绝 巧 弃 利

dào zéi wú yǒu　盗 贼 无 有

cǐ sān zhě yǐ wéi wén bù zú　此 三 者 以 为 文 不 足

gù lìng yǒu suǒ shǔ　故 令 有 所 属

jiàn sù bào pǔ shǎo sī guǎ yù　见 素 抱 朴 少 私 寡 欲

Reject holiness   forgo cleverness
The people will profit a hundredfold

Reject benevolence   forgo righteousness
The people will rediscover authentic kindness

Reject craftiness   forgo profit
There will be no thieves

These are three valuable rules
but more important is the foundation

Be simple
     like undyed silk   like the uncarved block

The self recedes
Desires soften

A religion emerged from the teachings of Laozi, Zhuangzi, and other early Daoists, but you wouldn't have expected it from the opening line of this verse. Laozi states, quite clearly, *reject holiness.* I suppose that this shouldn't come as a surprise. All religions seem to have become divorced from the spirituality espoused by their founders. If Jesus of Nazareth was at all the person described by Paul in the New Testament, I shudder to think what Jesus would think of American Christian nationalists and the Catholic Church's cultivation of pedophilia. Actually, Jesus was probably much more the anti-Roman revolutionary zealot hinted at by Mark and James than the sanitized Jesus Christ served up by Paul, so that's good. What would Mohammed make of the Taliban and the Saudi royals? What would Siddhartha Gotama make of people claiming to be—actually, physically—reborn by following his teachings about living honestly?

Reject benevolence and *reject cleverness* are the other two guidelines that open this verse, and these three *valuable rules* are clear and simple. Laozi is giving fairly basic life advice of the sort seen in many ancient documents, including the Ten Commandments of Christianity, the Five Pillars of Islam, and the Four Noble Truths and the Eightfold Path of Buddhism. But rules are only needed when people have drifted from the straight and narrow. It is the straight and narrow itself—the Path, the Way, the Dao— that should be the foundation of our behavior, argues, Laozi. To be on the Path is to be simple—*like undyed silk, like the uncarved block*—and rules are only required to return us to the best versions of ourselves when we stray.

The *uncarved block* is one of Laozi's recurring images. In this verse, undyed silk is added for emphasis. The uncarved block represents the uncomplicated person with unlimited potential. Consider an artistic ethic infused with simplification rather than complication. Some art is created by a process of adding to: layers of paint to a canvas, for example. Other art can be imagined as a process of taking from: layers of marble or jade carved from a block. The process of taking away reveals the perfect sculpture that was hiding inside the block. The process of simplifying a life, stripping away all the frills, fluff, and flounce, can reveal the simple beauty of the person within.

And this is especially true when the mind is simplified; cleared, de-cluttered. *The self recedes. Desires soften.*

VERSE 20. THE OUTSIDER

Sister Margaret's sheep at the convent farm, Meru, Kenya

20　二十

jué xué wú yōu
绝学无忧

wéi zhī yú ā xiāng qù jǐ hé
唯之与阿相去几何

shàn zhī yú è xiāng qù ruò hé
善之与恶相去若何

rén zhī suǒ wèi bù kě bù wèi
人之所畏不可不畏

huāng xī qí wèi yāng zāi
荒兮其未央哉

zhòng rén xī xī rú xiǎng tài láo
众人熙熙如享太牢

rú chūn dēng tái
如春登台

wǒ dú bó xī qí wèi zhào
我独泊兮其未兆

rú yīng ér zhī wèi hái
如婴儿之未孩

lěi lěi xī ruò wú suǒ guī
儽儽兮若无所归

zhòng rén jiē yǒu yú ér wǒ dú ruò yí
众人皆有余而我独若遗

wǒ yú rén zhī xīn yě zāi
我愚人之心也哉

dùn dùn xī sú rén zhāo zhāo wǒ dú hūn hūn
沌沌兮俗人昭昭我独昏昏

sú rén chá chá wǒ dú mēn mēn
俗人察察我独闷闷

zhòng rén jiē yǒu yǐ ér wǒ dú wán qiě bǐ
众人皆有以而我独顽且鄙

wǒ dú yì yú rén ér guì shí mǔ
我独异于人而贵食母

How different is a formal *yes* from an informal *yeah*?
How different is good from evil?

Should we fear what others fear?
It seems we always have—but what foolishness!

The crowds are thriving and happy
    as if at the Tailao festival
    as if basking on the summer terrace

Me? I am quiet and calm
    like a newborn babe still too young to giggle
And so very tired   and with nowhere to go

The crowds have an abundance   a surfeit
Me? I have nothing   I am confused   A fool

Most people seem bright   I seem dull
They seem to have purpose   I don't know...
    I drift about like a desolate ocean
    I blow around like a feckless wind

They seem skilled   useful
Me? I am clumsy

I am not like other people
I am nourished by the great mother

Something strange happened here, in both content and style. This verse is an outlier in the *Daodejing*, and its strangeness supports the judgment that the book is compiled from the sayings of multiple sages and the writings of multiple authors. If Laozi wrote this verse, he was in one heck of a mood. It is one of the most poetic verses in the *Daodejing* and the most introspective (or sardonic) and is wonderfully strange.

Laozi describes himself as *tired, and with nowhere to go*. He has nothing, is confused: a fool. He drifts about *like a desolate ocean*—my God!—and blows around *like a feckless wind*. Yikes. Everyone else is partying, as if at the Tailao Festival, but Loazi is not a part of the festivities. He is clumsy.

But perhaps there's some arrogance here too. Is Laozi looking at these partygoers with a little disdain? Is he judging them as trivial and unenlightened? I think he might be. Laozi has become an outsider, and we are led to understand that all those who become enlightened should expect similar experiences. Joining the minority who have seen behind the curtain can be difficult, because once you've seen the Wizard of Oz pulling the strings, there are new truths that you must confront. To see through the veil is to see the world with greater clarity. Everything changes for Neo when he takes the red pill and can see *The Matrix*.[15] Perhaps it is humility and perhaps it is arrogance, or perhaps it is a bit of both.

One of life's great fears is that of being different. We are a small group mammal that evolved complex social behavior in distant times. Our biological evolution has formed a deeply empathic, social creature replete with adaptations to communal living but also rife with exaptations and maladaptations to the same. Humans have evolved to come together in ways that are found in no other species, but people can also become sheeple. Laozi seeks balance. It is honorable to be a participating member of society, to obey the law, to respect one's leaders, but it is also necessary to be an individual: distinct, a dissenter, an outsider, if necessary.

But Laozi is at peace with these difficulties. No, he may not be able to fit in with society like others do and as perhaps he once did, but that's okay. He is *nourished by the great mother*—by connection to the Dao.

VERSE 21. BY THIS

Stages of the Zen enso circle representing the void, enlightenment, the cosmos

21　二十一

kǒng dé zhī róng wéi dào shì cōng	孔德之容惟道是从
dào zhī wéi wù wéi huǎng wéi hū	道之为物惟恍惟惚
hū xī huǎng xī qí zhōng yǒu xiàng	惚兮恍兮其中有象
huǎng xī hū xī qí zhōng yǒu wù	恍兮惚兮其中有物
yǎo xī míng xī qí zhōng yǒu jīng	窈兮冥兮其中有精
qí jīng shén zhēn	其精甚其
qí zhōng yǒu xìn	其中有信
zì gǔ jí jīn	自古及今
qí míng bù qù yǐ yuè zhòng fǔ	其名不去以阅众甫
wú hé yǐ zhī zhòng fǔ zhī zhuàng zāi	吾何以知众甫之状哉
yǐ cǐ	以此

Great virtue only comes from following the Path
The Path is indistinct and vague

Indistinct and vague   but at its center   shape
Indistinct and vague   but at its center   substance
Obscure   veiled   but within it   spirit
The spirit is true   and within it   trust

Known since ancient times
It is never forgotten
The ancestor of everything

How do I know it is the great ancestor?
By this

As if *by this* serves as some kind of explanation. Honestly, Laozi, are you even trying? *How do I know it is the great ancestor? By this.* Really?

Is Laozi asking us to have faith? It seems like he might be, and that would be a problem for me. Faith is one of the things I find disagreeable—about religion, politics, and anything else. I'm sorry, but faith is not an option. As Mark Twain said, "Faith is believing what you know ain't so," and it is one of the great turnoffs. If you want me to believe in something, you're going to have to explain it to me. Don't worry, I'm reasonably smart. If you can explain it, I'll probably get it. One of the things I love about the teachings of Laozi and the Buddha and mystics such as the Stoics is their avoidance of dogma, their aversion to faith, and their insistence that if their philosophy is not working for you, then don't bother with it . . .

. . . but Laozi is still struggling to describe the Dao. It is *indistinct and vague* but *with shape and substance*. It is *obscure* but has spirit and trust. It has been *known since ancient times*, never forgotten, and is *the ancestor of everything*. Fair enough, but we have to be honest: this verse doesn't really teach us anything, show us anything, or explain anything.

The approach is similar to the Buddhist idea of the koan, which is a riddle meant to stimulate insight. The most famous koan is probably "What is the sound of one hand clapping?" to which there is no correct answer per se, but there is the hope that the koan will engage enlightening ponderings on the physical properties of sound and the workings of the mind. One hand clapping makes no sound, but what do two hands clapping do? They compress air and cause the ear drum to vibrate, which excites neurons stimulating the brain to interpret this as a thing we call sound. Hearing is mostly about simulation in the brain. The world is lived in our minds.

How to explain to another person what they will think or feel when they begin to understand the workings of their mind? First, it is hard to describe your own experience of such a thing. Second, another person's path and discoveries will be different than yours. The approach, then, is an indication of where to look: a pointing at. Look for the Dao in your own mind. And how do we know it is the right place to be looking for the meaning of life?

By this.

VERSE 22. DAOIST BEATITUDES

Plum blossoms

22	二十二
qū zé quán wăng zé zhí	曲则全枉则直
wā zé yíng bì zé xīn	洼则盈敝则新
shăo zé dé duō zé huó	少则得多则惑
shì yĭ shèng rén bào yī wéi tiān xià shì	是以圣人抱一为天下式
bù zì jiàn gù míng bù zì shì gù zhāng	不自见故明不自是故彰
bù zì fá gù yŏu gōng bù zì jīn gù cháng	不自伐故有功不自矜故长
fū wéi bù zhēng gù tiān xià mò néng yú zhī zhēng	夫唯不争故天不莫能与之争
gŭ zhī suŏ wèi qū zé quán zhĕ	古之所谓曲则全者
qĭ xū yán zāi chéng quán ér guī zhī	岂虚言哉诚全而归之

Yield to become complete
Be twisted to be straight
Be emptied to be full
Be broken to be whole
Have little to gain much
Have too much and be restless

The wise cleave to the one
as their foundation

Not conceited   they shine
Not emphatic   they are reliable
Not boastful   their renown endures
and since they do not compete
they cannot be challenged

Why did the ancestors say
Yield to become complete?
Were these just empty words?
Indeed not!
To be complete is to return

Blessed are the meek, for they shall inherit the earth.
MATTHEW 5:5

The opening stanza gives a lovely sense of the value of developing resilience. Being twisted and broken is what happens to me on my rare visits to the gym. The body benefits from a good workout. Being emptied, hungry, and fasting every now and then can be good for your digestion. Being broke early in life teaches us the value of work. We must be tested and challenged in order to build the resilience to flourish in a capricious world. We must also be humble enough to be humbled from time to time. This too is necessary for growth.

The Eastern and Western religious and philosophical traditions are quite distinct, but they do overlap where they seek enlightenment and spirituality. My sense is that the Eastern religions open doors to the spiritual world more effectively than the Western religions, especially when they stay close to their philosophical roots. Christianity, for example, strikes me as a religion that might prevent people from finding spirituality: boredom in church as a kid, pedophiles in the news. This is the path to spirituality? I think not...

...but for some people, it seems that this is the path to spirituality. There is clearly a vast abundance of charlatans. The American Christian nationalists come immediately to mind. "God hates fags!" does not strike me as a gateway to spirituality, but some people do appear to find their spiritual selves through Christianity. They tote the baggage of strange (or ridiculous) ideas along with them (Noah's Ark, Jonah and the whale, talking snakes, etc.), but that's a separate matter.

It seems to me that you can pick any religion, philosophy, or mindset and use it as a gateway to the development of your own spirituality. I enjoy the image of the Dao as a guiding Path or Way and as a sense of the physics of the cosmos, the evolution of life, and the ecological and evolutionary connectedness of everything. It locates me in space and time. Yes, I am small and insignificant compared to the past-present-future cosmos, but then I *am* the past-present-future cosmos: a mote, yet a multitude, and all that.

The Bible has some pretty dubious passages, but the Sermon on the Mount is great in any culture or context. Daoism (the religion) has some pretty hokey ideas, but the *Daodejing* is full of wisdom. These convergences are sweet spots where, independently, and in different places and times, some of the world's great seekers of spirituality found common ground. Irrespective of the direction from which you approach them, these convergences are worth a close look. *Yield to be complete. To complete is to return.*

VERSE 23. EMULATE NATURE AND BE ONE WITH LOSS

Cloghane Estuary, Dingle Peninsula, Ireland

23　二十三

xī yán zì rán	希	言	自	然		
gù piāo fēng bù zhōng cháo	故	飘	风	不	终	朝
zhòu yǔ bù zhōng rì	骤	雨	不	终	日	
shú wèi cǐ zhǐ tiān dì	孰	为	此	者	天	地
tiān dì shàng bù néng jiǔ	天	地	尚	不	能	久
ér kuàng yú rén hū	而	况	于	人	乎	
gù cóng shì yú dào zhě tóng yú dào	故 从 事 于 道 者 同 于 道
dé zhě tóng yú dé	德 者 同 于 德
shī zhě tóng yú shī	失 者 同 于 失
tóng yú dào zhě dào yì lè dé zhī	同 于 道 者 道 亦 乐 得 之
tóng yú dé zhě dé yì lè dé zhī	同 于 德 者 德 亦 乐 得 之
tóng yú shī zhě shī yì lè dé zhī	同 于 失 者 失 于 乐 得 之
xìn bù zú yān yǒu bù xìn yān	信 不 足 焉 而 不 信 焉

Nature is not a blabbermouth
    A storm doesn't go on all morning
    A cloudburst doesn't gush all day
What makes the wind and the rain?
Heaven and earth
    So if heaven and earth aren't long-winded
    surely people don't need to be

Engage with the Path to be one with the Path
Engage with virtue to be one with virtue
Engage with loss to be one with loss

Be one with the Path to master the Path
Be one with virtue to master virtue
Be one with loss to master loss

If you don't show trust
you won't find trust

The *Daodejing* was not initially written in eighty-one verses; it was a single continuous text. It was divided into verses later, and the division is sometimes questionable. Sometimes it seems as though two verses should be read as one. Other times it seems as though a verse should be divided into two verses. One striking example is verse 42, and another is here. This verse has two significant themes: one in the first stanza and a separate one in the last three stanzas.

1. *Emulate nature.* This is a common theme of the *Daodejing.* A fancy modern word for this is "biomimicry." Velcro is a great example of a technology developed using biomimicry. Its hooks and grips were inspired by the weedy herb common burdock. Scientists are attempting many technologies that mimic to improve human-developed gadgets, but copying gadgets is not where the greatest potential lies. The most important ways we can emulate nature is not in the things of nature but rather in the *ways* of nature. Nature operates with productivity and complexity without fuss and without waste. Nature holds all the secrets to sustainability. We live in nature; we are a part of it. All we need to do is to pay attention.

And in conversation, remember: Nature is not a blabbermouth. A storm doesn't go on all morning. A cloudburst doesn't gush all day, so surely you don't need to.

2. *Be one with loss.* The second part of this verse switches to a different theme. Here, suddenly, is an unexpectedly challenging concept: *Engage with loss to be one with loss* and *Be one with loss to master loss.* This seems awfully negative. What does it mean?

In 2016, Albert Woodfox was released from Louisiana's barbaric Angola prison after forty-three years of solitary confinement.[16] Prison is a punishment. Solitary confinement is a prison punishment. Most people suffer serious mental pathologies after only days in solitary. Being left alone with nothing but your own human mind is a terribly dangerous thing. To survive requires incredible skill and fortitude. Woodfox controlled his desires. No smoking. No drinking. He tried to avoid craving sleep, sleeping for only three hours a day. In order to resist dependence on the guards, he never asked for the light to be turned off. He trained his mind to cope with his near-impossible environment and refused to let the racist American South rob him of his sanity. Albert Woodfox mastered injustice, fear, and his own mind, and he mastered loss. If you can engage with loss, be one with it, and master it, what, then, can be taken from you?

VERSE 24. SHORT SHRIFT FOR BRAGGARTS

The Great Basin outside Winnemucca, Nevada

24   二十四

qǐ zhě bù lì   企者不立

kuà zhě bù xíng   跨者不行

zì jiàn zhě bù míng   自见者不明

zì shì zhě bù zhāng   自是者不彰

zì fá zhě wú gōng   自伐者无功

zì jīn zhě bù cháng   自矜者不长

qí zài dào yě yuē yú shí zhuì xíng   其在道也曰余食赘形

wù huò ě zhī   物或恶之

gù yǒu dào zhě bù chǔ   故有道者不处

He who tiptoes will be unsteady
He who strides will not walk far
The opinionated are not bright
The self-righteous are unaware
Braggarts achieve little of value
Boasters are eventually exposed

To the Dao such people are
    leftover food
    pointless exertion
Things that the world despises

So why imitate them?
Followers of the Path do not indulge

One shows the faults of others like chaff winnowed in the wind, but one conceals one's own faults as a cunning gambler conceals his dice.
ATTRIBUTED TO THE BUDDHA IN
THE DHAMMAPADA (v. 352)

Why do you see the speck in your neighbor's eye, but not the log in your own eye?
ATTRIBUTED TO JESUS OF NAZARETH
IN *MATTHEW* 7:3

Here's a nice simple verse with straightforward advice on how to live a calm, honest life. First, remain grounded: *He who tiptoes will be unsteady.* And don't overstretch or over-promise: *He who strides will not walk far.* Check your self-righteous indignations. It is not a sign that you are extra right about something but that you are unaware. Try to be a humble listener rather than a self-righteous talker.

Self-promoters are much more obvious to others than to themselves and often appear unaware of their transparency. They seem to think they are cleverly manipulating people and that nobody has noticed. I say "they," of course, but mean "we" and "I." We are quick to react to the faults of others while failing to see our own.

Laozi is scathing in his rejection of braggarts. They are *leftover food* and *pointless exertion.* Ouch. They are *things that the world despises.* That's strong stuff and quite humiliating for me when I look back on a life of Machiavellian antics that I now realize weren't as subtle and secretive as I had imagined. Was I really that transparent? Yes, Steve, you were. Ouch. The *Daodejing's* call for living with honesty and humility is spelled out starkly here. *Braggarts achieve little of value.*

The saying "You never learn much by listening to yourself" has been attributed to George Clooney and many` others, but it is an ancient idea, and whoever said it first (probably not George Clooney), it is a good saying. The tendency for us to see the faults of others ahead of our own is revealed in our tendency to interrupt conversations. Have you ever noticed how some people seem to engage in discussions as if they were in a competition? They listen not for the sake of learning but instead to find a gap in the discussion where they can insert their next point. These people are very frustrating, and it is insulting that they don't seem to be taking heed of anything you say. I'm sure you've noticed it: it is common, possibly the norm, and it is annoying as hell. Heaven forbid that we should be guilty of such behavior ourselves . . .

VERSE 25. THE END OF CHAOS

Heron

25 二十五

yǒu wù hún chéng xiān tiān dì shēng	有物混成先天地生
jì xī liáo xī dú lì bù gǎi	寂兮寥兮独立不改
zhōu xíng ér bù dài	周行而不殆
kě yǐ wéi tiān xià mǔ	可以为天下母
wú bù zhī qí míng	吾不知其名
jiàng zì zhī yuē dào	强字之曰道
jiàng wéi zhī míng yuē dà	强为之名曰大
dà yuē shì shì yuē yuǎn yuǎn yuē fǎn	大曰逝逝曰远远曰反
gù dào dà tiān dà dì dà rén yì dà	故道大天大地大人亦大
yù zhōng yǒu sì dà ér rén jū qí yī yān	域中有四大而人居其一焉
rén fǎ dì dì fǎ tiān tiān fǎ dào	人法地地法天天法道
dào fǎ zì rán	道法自然

Something came to end the chaos
before the formation of heaven and earth
Silent
Empty
Standing alone unchanged
Everywhere
Always
Call it the mother of everything under heaven

Great means always flowing
Always flowing leads to reaching far
Reaching far results in returning to the root

Thus Dao is great
Heaven is great
The world is great
The king can be great

There are four greats and the king can be one of them

People emulate the earth
earth emulates heaven
and heaven emulates the Dao
The Dao simply is

The "great" ontological argument has been going on for centuries, which is an awful lot of wasted argument, but here goes for nothing. If the universe was formed from a singularity, in a Big Bang, what came before the singularity? God, obviously. But what came before God? Oh. Some Christians claim that St. Anselm of Canterbury wrapped the whole argument up by claiming God as "a being than which no greater can be conceived." Okay, so if that proves to you that God exists, just go with it. Laozi, to be fair, says something similar here with his own vague notions of the origins of the cosmos. The universe was without form and was void—Chaos—and then Dao said, "Let there be light!" And there was light. Everyone has their own idea of what came first, but mustn't something always come before something?

Whatever came to end the chaos, it eventually found its flow. One of the essences of the Dao is the way it constantly flows, like a river, and constantly changes and renews, like a bellows, pumping, finding its balance, following and creating its path. *Everything changes* is one of the great wisdoms of the East. Pointing at this is to point at anatta, the One, the no-self. Life flows into you, swirls as you, transiently, and then flows out of you back into the cosmos, *always flowing, . . . reaching far, . . . returning to the root.*

And then there's the matter of Laozi and his kings: a paradox found in a number of verses. Laozi gives lots of advice to leaders and their subjects, but he seems to have never considered the possibility of functional self-rule. Here, Laozi challenges the king to rule with as little interference as possible, to let the people live naturally, in community, but not autonomously. The *Daodejing* is not a product of the modern era, and we cannot make it so. The quatrain *the Dao is great, heaven is great, the world is great*, and *the king can be great* seems so clunky now in a world that has democracies, but although Laozi was ahead of his time (and ours in many ways), he had his blind spots.

I do love the last line. *Dao fa ziran*. We have translated *ziran* elsewhere (Chapters 1 and 2 and verse 17) as "nature" and "naturally" and discussed its more literal translation as "self-so," or "of-its-own," and *ziran* comes into its own here. Whatever your views of governance may be, the ways of nature are primary. Everything comes from nature, returns to nature, and follows the way of nature. *Dao fa ziran*. The Dao simply is.

VERSE 26. BE STOIC

From the back of the California zephyr near Granby, Colorado

26　二十六

zhòng wéi qīng gēn	重 为 轻 根
jìng wéi zào jūn	静 为 躁 君
shì yǐ shèng rén zhōng rì xíng	是 以 圣 人 终 日 行
bù lí qīng zhòng	不 离 轻 重
suī yǒu róng guān	虽 有 荣 观
yān chǔ chāo rán	燕 处 超 然
nài hé wàn chéng zhī zhǔ	奈 何 万 乘 之 主
ér yǐ shēn qīng tiān xià	而 以 身 轻 天 下
qīng zé shī gēn	轻 则 失 根
zào zé shī jūn	躁 则 失 君

Steadiness is the master of frivolity
Stillness is the ruler of impatience

The wise stay with the baggage wagons
when they travel
They may see magnificent sights
but remain satisfied with the simple
like a swallow in a nest

Why would a powerful ruler
    a commander of ten thousand chariots
rush about like a fool?

By frivolity   mastery is lost
By impatience   the ruler is deposed

So other people hurt me? That's their problem. Their character and actions are not mine. What is done to me is ordained by nature, what I do by my own.

Don't ever forget . . . That you are part of nature and no one can prevent you from speaking and acting in harmony with it, always.
MARCUS AURELIUS, *MEDITATIONS*, 5.25, 2.29

Daoism has very little in common with most Western philosophy, and one might be tempted to see a strict East-West divide between world philosophies except that some of the commonalities are striking. Plato's writings about Socrates—such as "Know Thyself" (see verse 33)— are one example, and another is Stoicism, an ancient Greek philosophy that emphasizes logic, humility, equanimity, and living according to the guidance of nature. Stoicism originated in Greece but was adopted by many Romans, most famously Emperor Marcus Aurelius.

This verse has a decidedly Stoic ring to it. It is also quite a skillful poem in which the flow of logic introduced in the first stanza—*steadiness is the master* and *stillness is the ruler*—loops back in the last stanza: *mastery is lost* and *the ruler is deposed.*

Stoic philosophy emphasized the development of virtue as a pathway to happiness and resilience and might be crudely summed up as "virtue is the only good." The Stoics aimed to develop a mental toughness and equanimity that would allow them to endure pain and grief with patience and enjoy pleasure and joy with level-headedness. In short, the Stoic approach is similar to that advocated in the *Daodejing.*

The concept of stillness is also interesting and is the key component of Doaist meditation, a form of meditation that offers very little structure or instruction but simply advocates stillness of body and mind. The realization that the body and mind are one and are one with the cosmos can be felt in stillness. We might contrast this approach with that of Buddhism, which utilizes more direct techniques and teachings such as mantras and koans to bring about awakening. It is noteworthy that a key step in the formation of Zen Buddhism, now predominant in Japan and the West, was the merging of Mayahana Buddhism with Daoism in China.

VERSE 27. TEACHER AND STUDENT

Bottomland field beside the Wabash River in Carroll County, Indiana

27　二十七

shàn xíng wú chè jì	善行无辙迹
shàn yán wú xiá zhé	善言无瑕谪
shàn shǔ bù yòng chóu cè	善数不用筹策
shàn bì wú guān jiàn ér bù kě kāi	善闭无关楗而不可开
shàn jiē wú shéng yāo ér bù kě jiě	善结无绳约而不可解
shì yǐ shèng rén	是以圣人
cháng shàn jiù rén gù wú qì rén	常善救人故无弃人
cháng shàn jiù wù gù wú qì wù	常善救物故无弃物
shì wèi xí míng	是谓袭明
gù shàn rén zhě bù shàn rén zhī shī	故善人者不善人之师
bù shàn rén zhě shàn rén zhī zī	不善人者善人之资
bù guì qí shī bù ài qí zī	不贵其师不爱
suī zhì dà mí	虽智大迷
shì wèi yāo miào	是谓要妙

A skilled tracker leaves no trace
A skilled speaker leaves no doubt
A skilled bookkeeper needs no gadgets

A well-made door needs no padlock
    and yet cannot be forced
A well-made binding needs no rope
    and yet cannot be loosened

The wise help everybody ignoring none
    saving everything
    wasting nothing
an inclusiveness that makes them luminous

Good people serve as teacher to those
    who need to learn
    who in turn
serve to help the teacher grow

Anyone who disrespects a teacher
    or undervalues a student
    may seem clever
but is on the wrong road

This is one valuable teaching of the Dao

Well-made things are valuable, as are deeds well done. Excellence is achieved by skilled people who have been properly trained. This verse suggests that Laozi sees the training of the skilled tracker, speaker, and bookkeeper as a community effort: it takes a village, they say.[17] *The wise help everybody, ignoring none.* The village trains people to do all the jobs of the village. Or, as the French saying goes, *Chacun son métier, et les moutons seront bien gardés* (Each to their role, and the sheep will be well guarded). Teachers are therefore highly valued, and this is not limited to professional teachers but also applies to all those who share their knowledge and skills with others. They help everybody, and *it makes them luminous.*

And just as students need teachers, so too do teachers need students. Being a learner helps people to develop into teachers, and thus teachers and students are interdependent. There is no great teaching without willing learners. A student might feign cleverness by scorning teachers or a teacher might act superior by disparaging students, but both of these behaviors reveal people who have strayed from the path. We all begin as students and should all develop into teachers, becoming, increasingly, teacher and student both.

The development of the perfect skills of the tracker, speaker, and bookkeeper, or of the artisan who builds the perfect-fitting door or perfect binding describes an important facet of *wuwei*. To do not-doing usually refers to the act of leaving a thing untouched or resisting the urge to meddle, but it also refers to the effortless action of an expert at work. Excellent work is never effortless, but it can seem to be thanks to superior skill. It is only possible once the effort of learning and training have been invested.

We sometimes refer to the phenomenon of being "in the zone," or in a state of flow, when we find ourselves performing tasks with unconscious ease. We find flow when the mind gets out of the way and lets the body act smoothly or when the mind and body are aligned to a task. We get lost in our work. Time seems to pass quickly, and the tennis shots we hit, the brush strokes we lay on the canvas, or the arpeggios we trace out on the keyboard have a touch of magic about them. Being in a state of flow, working with *wuwei*, will tend to produce things of quality and beauty.

Does this verse encapsulate the Dao? No, says Laozi. It is valuable, but it is just one practical little teaching.

VERSE 28. SUNLIGHT AND SHADOW

阴阳

阴阳

阴阳

Yin and yang in simplified characters, traditional characters, and seal script

28　二十八

zhī qí xióng shǒu qí cí wéi tiān xià xī	知 其 雄 守 其 雌 为 天 下 溪
wéi tiān xià xī cháng dé bù lí	为 天 下 溪 常 德 不 离
fù guī yú yīng ér	复 归 于 婴 儿
zhī qí bái shǒu qí hēi wéi tiān xià shì	知 其 白 守 其 黑 为 天 下 式
wéi tiān xià shì cháng dé bù tè	为 天 下 式 常 德 不 忒
fù guī yú wú jí	复 归 于 无 极
zhī qí róng shǒu qí rǔ tiān xià gǔ	知 其 荣 守 其 辱 为 天 下 谷
wéi tiān xià gǔ cháng dé nǎi zú	为 天 下 谷 常 德 乃 足
fù guī yú pǔ	复 归 于 朴
pǔ sǎn zé wéi qì	朴 散 则 为 器
shèng rén yòng zhī zé wéi guān zhǎng	圣 人 用 之 则 为 官 长
gù dà zhì bù gē	故 大 制 不 割

Know the masculine
but cleave to the feminine
Be the mountain stream of the world
Being the mountain stream
your virtue is secure
and you return to infancy

Know the light
but cleave to the dark
Be an example to the world
Being an example
your virtue will not fail
and you return to boundlessness

Know your honor
but cleave to your humility
Be the river valley of the world
Being the river valley
your virtue will be inexhaustible
and you become like the uncarved block

The uncarved block can be worked
and shaped into useful things
The wise are turned into leaders
without any carving

We return to the themes of yin-yang and the uncarved block. The first three stanzas reinforce the tendency of the Dao to turn toward the yin rather than the yang, to lean into the feminine rather than the masculine, to stand in the dark (shadow) rather than bask in the light (bright), to embrace humility rather than grasp at honor. This invocation of the yin is a revolutionary idea and one of the most important concepts of the *Daodejing*. Yin and yang are inseparable opposites of a single whole. They arise together, and Daoism does not seek to separate them but does take the unusual step of foregrounding yin over yang, an important shift of focus. Strength does not come only from the masculine, the light, honor, but also comes from the feminine, the dark, humility. Your virtue is secure when you act like the mountain stream of the world seeking the lowest places.

This verse has a lovely rendering of the concept of the uncarved block. Things and people are generally improved by simplifying them, not by complicating them. Some of this might only become obvious as you reach the later edges of middle age and tiptoe toward old age. Life is not improved by adding clutter. You don't need a flashier car or a bigger house. Simplify. Slow down. Send a bunch of that crap to the kids or to Goodwill. Stop seeking raises and promotions: that's a young fool's game, and you are no longer a young fool. Improve yourself like a sculptor not by adding to but by taking from. Clutter and unwanted bulk are carved from the block. The finished product is lesser in size, but its simplicity may retain a certain elegance. But this is not the only image of the uncarved block here. The last line of this verse is interesting. *The wise are turned into leaders without any carving.* It is prefaced a few lines earlier: *become like the uncarved block.* What does this mean? If the perfect sculpture resides within the uncarved block, surely this perfection should be released by carving, but in carving one sculpture all other possible sculptures have been lost. Carved, the block is imbued with more direct value, but all other potential sculptures have been nullified. And there can be much more beauty in the uncarved block than with any possible carved statue. Consider the mental trick of moving backward in time from the uncarved block rather than forward. The uncarved block of wood began as a tree. The tree was part of a forest, an ecosystem with diverse populations living in complex communities. The uncarved block was most beautiful when it was still part of the uncut forest.

Leaning toward the yin of things rather than the yang and considering the simplicity and perfection of things in their untrammeled, undeveloped, unmined, unlogged, unpolluted (uncarved) state is a central premise of the *Daodejing*.

VERSE 29. THE PATHOLOGY OF CONTROL

Celery Bog Nature Area, West Lafayette, Indiana

29　二十九

jiāng yù qǔ tiān xià ér wéi zhī	将欲取天下而为之
wú jiàn qí bù dé yǐ	吾见其不得已
tiān xià shén qì bù kě wéi yě	天下神器不可为也
wéi zhě bài zhī zhí zhě shī zhī	为者败之执者失之
fū wù huò xíng huò suí	夫物或行或随
huò xū huò chuī	或歔或吹
huò jiàng huò yíng	或强或赢
huò cuò huò huī	或挫或隳
shì yǐ shèng rén	是以圣人
qù shén qù shē qù tài	去甚去奢去泰

Conquer the world and change it?
It can't be done
The world is sacred
it can't be controlled
Try to defeat it
you will lose it

The way of nature is
to lead   but also to follow
to be calm   and yet sometimes agitated
to be strong   but not the strongest
to feel safe   and then suddenly frightened

The wise limit wastefulness and pride
and temper the desire to control

If you listen to technology-minded folks for long enough you'd be forgiven for concluding that, as I once heard a seminar speaker say, "There's an engineering solution for every environmental problem." The climate is out of control, and we must get it back under control, except that it was never ours to control. This river or that lake might burst its banks in a flood, and people's houses might be damaged: the river must be controlled. The population is out of control: we must produce more food, except that producing food the way we currently produce it would further damage soils that are already degraded and draw down water resources that are already depleted.

The one thing that might be valuable to be able to control is our desire to control.

One of the most fascinating mistakes people make when trying to imagine a more sustainable future is to confuse conservation with efficiency. Let's say we want to conserve gasoline. The obvious way to do this would be to drive less, but wait, there's another option: we could get a more efficient car. This would allow us to drive just as much as before and still conserve gasoline. Well, it would allow that, I suppose, but what we actually tend to do is drive the more efficient car farther. And why shouldn't we? It is more efficient, which means it is cheaper to run. This doesn't seem like a big deal until everyone does the same thing and many more miles are driven overall. And so, more roads are needed. And so, more cars are needed, more efficient cars, mind you, but they need more tires, more paint, more steel, more plastics, and so on. And as everything gets more efficient and we continue the pretense of sustainability, the consumption of everything increases, including the gasoline we had intended to save. Conservation and efficiency are not the same thing at all. Conservation conserves. Efficiency consumes. Indeed, efficiency is the heartbeat of innovation, progress, and economic growth. Curtailing growth requires us to slow down and do less, not try to cheat and game the system.

What we need is not urgency, technical fixes, or automated solutions. We don't need to wake up, get active, get busy, and save the planet. We don't need to make new gadgets, new machines, more efficient planes, new ways of capturing carbon dioxide, biogas, hydrogen fuel cells, recycled bags, better computers, finer light bulbs . . .

We don't need to do any of this, and we certainly don't need to do any of it in a hurry. What we need to do is less, more slowly, and *temper the desire to control. Conquer the world and change it? It can't be done.*

VERSE 30. THE PATHOLOGY OF DOMINATION

Re-created Longhouses at Prophetstown State Park, Battleground, Indiana

30　三十

yǐ dào zuǒ rén zhǔ zhě	以道佐人主者
bù yǐ bīng jiàng tiān xià	不以兵强天下
qí shì hǎo hái	其事好还
shī zhē suǒ chǔ jīng jí shēng yān	师之所处荆棘生焉
jūn zhī hòu bì yǒu xiōng nián	军之后必有凶年
shàn yǒu guǒ ér yǐ	善有果而已
bù gǎn yǐ qǔ jiàng	不敢以取强
guǒ ér wù jīn	果而勿矜
guǒ ér wù fá	果而勿伐
guǒ ér wù jiāo	果而勿骄
guǒ ér bù dé yǐ	果而不得已
guǒ ér wù jiàng	果而勿强
wù zhuàng zé lǎo shì wèi bù dào	物壮则老是谓不道
bù dào zǎo yǐ	不道早已

Controlling by force of arms
is in opposition to the Dao
It invites retribution

Where armies bivouac thorn bushes grow
Where armies clash harvests fail

The wise get results and then withdraw
They don't presume to take by force
They get results without bragging or boasting
     without arrogance
Results only as a last resort
Results without intimidation

We grow strong and then grow old
but we are not the Path
     on the Path   at best   a piece
and what is not the Path must die

If control is a pathology, then domination is a madness. Shock and awe. Overwhelming force. We don't like to just win and have our own way; we like to win big. We don't like to only control; we like to dominate. That this is a horrible way to be as well as a horrible mistake is yet another obvious lesson that seems to elude us.

This is the first of a number of verses in the *Daodejing* railing against militarism, force, and war. Laozi proclaims a deep-seated pacifism. He is not so naive as to expect war to end, and he gives practical strategic and tactical advice where necessary, but he is always against war. The statements *where armies bivouac thorn bushes grow* and *where armies clash harvests fail* are serious indictments of war and couldn't be more clear. War defiles nature and society far beyond the scope of any single battle.

This verse goes beyond war itself and addresses domination. Not only is it obvious that *controlling by force of arms is in opposition to the Dao* and therefore an ethical mistake but it is also a strategic one because *it invites retribution*. The colonized always rebel, violently if they must. The attempt to dominate is an arrogant objective and a fool's errand.

If they must fight, the wise do so for clear practical reasons. They fight because they must, and they honor their enemy. They neither brag nor boast. There is no tactical or strategic advantage to be gained by bragging. All it does is goad the enemy and increase the likelihood of retribution. If there must be fighting, it should be strictly to attain results, and we should seek *results only as a last resort*.

There is an important personal and political message here, because it is not only in military conflicts that people seek to dominate. People try to dominate other people in relationships and in the workplace. People hope for their political party not only to win an election but also to dominate the opposition. This is always a mistake. The wise get results and then withdraw. Observers of the Dao understand that there is no control, no long-term domination, and no ultimate victory. We can follow the path, but we are not the path itself. We are a part of the path. It goes on. We individuals are fleeting. We die. How could we possibly dominate for more than a moment?

VERSE 31. THE PATHOLOGY OF VICTORY

Crane

31 三十一

fū jiā bīng zhě bù xiáng zhī qì	夫 佳 兵 者 不 祥 之 器
wù huò è zhī	物 或 恶 之
gù yǒu dào zhě bù chǔ	故 有 道 者 不 处
jūn zǐ jū zé guì zuǒ	君 子 居 则 贵 左
yòng bīng zé guì yòu	用 兵 则 贵 右
bīng zhě bù xiáng zhī qì	兵 者 不 祥 之 器
fēi jūn zǐ zhī qì	非 君 子 之 器
bù dé yǐ ér yòng zhī	不 得 已 而 用 之
tián dàn wéi shàng	恬 淡 为 上
shèng ér bù měi	胜 而 不 美
ér měi zhī zhě shì lè shā rén	而 美 之 者 是 乐 杀 人
fū lè shā rén zhě	夫 乐 杀 人 者
zé bù kě dé zhì yú tiān xià yǐ	则 不 可 得 志 于 天 不 矣
jí shì shàng zuǒ xiōng shì shàng yòu	吉 事 尚 左 凶 事 尚 右
piān jiàng jūn jū zuǒ shàng jiàng jūn jū yòu	偏 将 军 居 左 上 将 军 居 右
yán yǐ sāng lǐ chǔ zhī	言 以 丧 礼 处 之
shā rén zhī zhòng yǐ bēi āi qì zhī	杀 人 之 众 以 悲 丧 泣 之
zhàn shèng yǐ sāng lǐ chǔ zhī	战 胜 以 丧 礼 处 之

Weapons no matter how beautiful
are the tools of violence
All men should detest them
Followers of the Dao should forswear them

In peacetime a gentleman favors his left
In war he wears weapons on his right

Weapons are the tools of violence
not the tools of a gentleman
They should only be used as a last resort
and with humility

In victory be solemn
To glorify victory is to glorify killing
If you glorify killing you can never be whole

The left side is fortunate
and the right side is stricken
The officer stands to the left of his commander
    in battles   and at funerals

When people have been killed
hear their pitiful cries of sorrow
Treat victory as a funeral

Laozi completes a homily on war here by arguing that when two sides fight, they have both already lost. There can be no stable resolution to rivalry through violent conflict. Fighting only makes any sense at all in self defense: *Weapons . . . should only be used as a last resort and with humility*. They are worn on the right, yang, side of the body. Most people wield a sword with their right, yang, hand. *The right side is stricken*, and *the left side is fortunate*. In peacetime we favor the yin, the go-to pole of the Dao.

Glorifying war makes sense, of course, to leaders. Those in power have always believed that it was necessary to be able to get large numbers of people to kill for them. So, making heroes of warriors also makes sense. What better way to get people to *want* to do this than by offering badges of status? The first stanza refers to the wearing of weapons in public, brandishing them as fashion statements and status symbols. Laozi is having none of it: *Weapons, no matter how beautiful, are the tools of violence. All men should detest them.*

The Buddha said, "Hatred cannot be cured by hatred." A military victory can never change the moral landscape. Compromise, agreement, and the recognition of shared humanity are goals to strive for, and none of these can be won by force. Yes, life is a constant struggle to make the world a better place and to make lives happier and more fulfilling, and we should engage in that struggle, but there is no ultimate victory to be had. The path needs constant shaping and always will. There can be no victory. *Treat victory as a funeral.*

How can we be open and honest and how can we reach equanimity when we glory in death? Striving for war, for glory in battle, is an extreme example of the *desire* that Laozi speaks of so often in the *Daodejing* and warns us against. If this particular desire is a part of your mindset, you have a mental pathology that needs to be tempered. *If you glorify in killing, you can never be whole.* Much of it, of course, can come from one's society. Nationalism is a pathology when a country worships the exploits of its military. It will lead the citizens of a country to glorify its "brave soldiers" who go off to fight a "noble war" against an "evil dictator" or "evil ideology." Our military heroes are agents of death, and we spend their lives cheaply. The greater courage is to resist this pathology, refuse to participate, and speak truth to power.

VERSE 32. THE FOREST
FOR THE TREES

The Rhizosphere

32　三十二

dào cháng wú míng	道常无名
pǔ suī xiǎo tiān xià mò néng chén yě	朴虽小天下莫能臣也
hóu wáng ruò néng shǒu zhī	侯王若能守之
wàn wù jiāng zì bīn	万物将自宾
tiān dì xiāng hé yǐ jiàng gān lòu	天地相合以降甘露
mín mò zhī lìng ér zì jūn	民莫之令而自均
shǐ zhì yǒu míng	始制有名
míng yì jì yǒu	名亦既有
fū yì jiāng zhī zhǐ	夫亦将知止
zhī zhǐ kě yǐ bù dài	知止可以不殆
pì dào zhī zài tiān xià	譬道之在天下
yóu chuān gǔ zhī yú jiāng hǎi	犹川谷之于江海

The Dao is eternally nameless
The uncarved block   Minuscule
and yet beyond the scope of heaven and earth

If leaders could only abide by it
everything would pay homage to them
    heaven and earth would rejoice
    sweet dew would fall
    citizens
    without needing to be coerced
    would live in harmony

But we split the block
and give the pieces names
    to control
    to govern
When the names multiply it's time to stop
If you know when to stop you are safe

The Dao   to the world
    is as the stream to the valley
    is as the river to the ocean

There are some people I'd love to bring to the modern world. Charles Darwin is top of my list. Imagine showing him how DNA and RNA complete his theory of evolution. Or imagine showing Galileo images from the space telescopes...

Laozi is wondering about the Dao again, and I get a very real sense of him pondering the cosmos here: *minuscule and yet beyond the scope of heaven and earth.* What fun it would be to give him a microscope so he could see the vast abundance of microbes in soil or a telescope so he could see stars and galaxies invisible to the unaided eye. His knowledge of the physical sciences was much less than ours, but he shared our sense of wonder. Laozi grasped both the hugeness and the smallness of the cosmos and sensed that it was all linked. He could see the forest and had a sense of reverence and awe for it even through the obscuring tangle of the trees. What fun it would be to show him the modern world.

Science is at its best when working on counterintuitive problems. It is intuitively obvious that the world is flat with a firmament of stars above, but science shows us that Earth is a pretty ordinary sphere orbiting a pretty ordinary star: the truth is often counterintuitive. The power of science often comes from reducing complex problems down to measurable parts, solving for those measurable parts, and then extrapolating back to the complex problem. We call this reductionist science, and it is how we have been able to figure out so many counterintuitive problems. But there is danger here. Science drives us to find out more and more about what's inside the uncarved block. We split it so that we can study its inner workings. Biologists reduce organisms down to their component cells. Cell biologists reduce cells down to their component molecules. Molecular biologists show how the biochemical machinery of life builds cells and organisms. Science reveals great beauty, but it can be the catalyst of hubris because its power can be unleashed in a desire to control. If control is incomplete, we split the block yet further and further as we seek better and better control—but some things are better left untouched.

Ecologists study things such as nutrient uptake by trees, fungal degradation of deadwood, and the sociobiology of deer and frogs. They extrapolate these findings to frame a better understanding of how forests work, and as a result of thousands of studies we know an awful lot about forest ecology. We know a lot about what's inside the uncarved block that is the forest. For some people, this deeper understanding of the functioning of forests can give them a fuller sense of the beauty of the forest, and that's good, but we need to rein in those who use detailed knowledge of forests to turn them into board feet.

VERSE 33. KNOW THYSELF

Building site, Addis Ababa, Ethiopia

33　三十三

zhī rén zhě zhì	知 人 者 智
zì zhī zhě míng	自 知 者 明
shèng rén zhě yǒu lì	胜 人 者 有 力
zì shèng zhě qiáng	自 胜 者 强
zhī zú zhě fù	知 足 者 富
qiáng xíng zhě yǒu zhì	强 行 者 有 志
bù shī qí suǒ zhě jiǔ	不 失 其 所 者 久
sǐ ér bù wáng zhě shòu	死 而 不 亡 者 寿

To know others is to be wise
To know yourself is to be enlightened
To master others takes force
To master yourself takes strength

To be content is to be rich
Be persistent   develop willpower
hold your place   remain steady
and you will endure

To die remembered   undefeated
is close enough to immortality

Know Thyself | Nothing to Excess | Surety Brings Ruin

Nosce te Ipsum (γνῶθι σ(ε)αυτόν), Know Thyself, was the first of three maxims inscribed in the forecourt of the Temple of Apollo in Delphi. The phrase has been popularly attributed to Socrates (470–399 BCE) in Plato's *Dialogues*, which were written around the same time as the *Daodejing*. Lots of original philosophy and other amazing cultural pieces were created around this time. Herodotus wrote *Histories* around 430 BCE. The Parthenon was completed in 438 BCE. Art and architecture were beginning to flourish in the late Zhou dynasty. Exchanges between China and Europe were not well established until after about 200 BCE, when the Silk Road began to link the Roman Empire and the Han dynasty, but it is tempting to think that much was shared between East and West long before then.

Improving the knowledge of self has been one of the great challenges of philosophy in all times and all places. You wouldn't think it would be that hard. Our self is, after all, the thing we spend the most time with and also the thing we spend the most time thinking about. Despite this, honest self-knowledge is difficult to develop and probably rather rare. We find it easier to make honest appraisals of others than we do of ourselves. Of course, since it is our self that's thinking about our self, perhaps we should expect its conclusions to be self-serving. *To know yourself is to be enlightened*, says Laozi, and *to master yourself takes strength*. Part of the trick of knowing yourself—your self—is to recognize that there is no such singular thing. No wonder it is hard to master. Mastery tends to imply gaining control, but the idea here is that self-mastery comes from surrendering control. The concept is different to the similar-seeming idea in the Abrahamic faiths, where one might surrender to God. This is not a surrendering to but instead is a releasing of. Understanding others requires intellect. Understanding yourself requires abnegation. Mastering others implies controlling them. Mastering yourself requires the strength to relinquish control.

Consider the unhappiness that can come from the struggle for wealth. Perhaps you're miserable trying to keep up with the Joneses. Perhaps you're miserable trying to satisfy various markers or milestones of success. (Or what you perceive to be someone else's milestones.) How much wealth is enough to make you happy? Strangely, the answer has less to do with the wealth than the enough. We perceive a gap between what we have and what we want. Let's call this the happiness gap. The wider the gap the more miserable we are, and the narrower the gap the happier we are. How to narrow the gap? We usually try to increase what we have. We buy stuff and we go out partying, and these things do narrow the gap—but only transiently. Soon enough, we need to buy more stuff and go out partying again. But the gap widens again. And the treadmill can accelerate. In order to keep closing the happiness gap, we need to buy more and better things and go to bigger and better parties. This is not sustainable. A more sustainable way to close the happiness gap is to reduce what we want. Reduce the denominator rather than increasing the numerator. Control the cravings and desires. *To be content* with what you have *is to be rich*. Always rich.

VERSE 34. A MOMENT OF REVELATION

From thirty-five thousand feet over Greenland

34 三十四

dà dào fàn xī qí kě zuǒ yòu	大道泛兮其可左右
wàn wù shì zhī yǐ shēng ér bù cí	万物恃之以生而不辞
gōng chéng ér bù míng yǒu	功成而不名有
yī yǎng wàn wù ér bù wéi zhǔ	衣养万物而不为主
cháng wú yù kě míng yú xiǎo	常无欲可名於小
wàn wù guī yān	万物归焉
ér bù wéi zhǔ kě míng wéi dà	而不为主可名为大
yǐ qí zhōng bù zì wéi dà	以其终不自为大
gù néng chéng qí dà	故能成其大

The great Way is wide   in flood
   flowing left   flowing right
Everything depends on it for life
It gives freely   sparing nothing
It clothes and nourishes everything
but makes no claim on anything

It has no needs   no desires
Call it small
Everything returns to it   unbidden
Call it great

The wise do not claim to be greater than anything
which is why they can become great

I really love these verses that Laozi throws in every now and then in which he seems to just step back, look at the world, and go "Wow." He tries to describe the Dao, but what he's feeling cannot be put into words. The Dao becomes a river: *The great way is wide, in flood, flowing left, flowing right.* It becomes a more encompassing vision of nature that *gives freely* and *clothes and nourishes everything.* It becomes the cosmos, both *small* and *great.*

Moments of revelation are some of the pivotal stories of religion. Muhammad had a sequence of revelations. In the first of these the angel Jibril (Gabriel) gave him the first passages of the Quran. Saul of Tarsus, a persecutor of Christians, had a revelation on the road to Damascus and became Saint Paul, the architect of the Christian faith. Arjuna had a revelation of Krishna, an avatar of Lord Vishnu, who guided him to follow his true nature through selfless action during battle in the "Righteous War" recounted in the Bhagavad Gita. The word "revelation" means to reveal the presence of God. The sight seen or the event witnessed is of such profundity that it could not, the observant would believe, have happened but for God.

But revelation is open to us all, theist and atheist alike, irrespective of creed or philosophy. During a quiet walk in the woods, the sky clears (or not), and the trees somehow look different: more luminous. The scene is somehow and mysteriously enlivened. Riding a motorcycle across a wide-open landscape, the fields seem somehow sharper: they move in slow motion, although you and the bike are tearing through the countryside. Playing piano, the piece you have recently mastered suddenly becomes easy: your hands flash over the keys without having to be shown the way. Enlightenment? Awakening? A simple, neurological sense of "flow?" When we are sufficiently calm, centered, we can all enter this beautiful state. The world *is wide, in flood, flowing left, flowing right.*

This verse closes by linking the great flowing Dao to ethics. If the Dao, which is so overwhelmingly powerful, *flowing left, flowing right,* while it *nourishes everything* can be humble, why can't you? If the Dao and *everything* that *depends on it for life* has *no needs, no desires,* why should you? Resisting the urge to master others is true greatness. The wise act with the restraint and humility of the Dao. They do not claim to be greater than anything, which, paradoxically, is what makes them great.

VERSE 35. CONTENTMENT OVER DESIRE

Farm outside Hoopestown, Illinois

35　三十五

zhí dà xiàng tiān xià wàng	执大象天下往
wàng ér bù hài ān píng tài	往而不害安平太
lè yú ěr guò kè zhǐ	乐与饵过客止
dào zhī chū kǒu dàn hū qí wú wèi	道之出口淡乎其无味
shì zhī bù zú jiàn	视之不足见
tīng zhī bù zú wén	听之不足闻
yòng zhī bù zú jì	用之不足既

Hold onto the great image
and let the world come to you
It will come quietly and peacefully

Fine music and exotic food
are passing pleasures
They attract passersby

The Path boasts no great speeches
no exotic flavors
no dramatic vistas
no grand music

but you can never have too much of it

Aristippus (435–356 BCE) coined the term *hedonia* for the peak experiences of pleasure that come from enjoying life to the full: thrill-seeking, satisfying cravings, fulfilling desires. Aristotle (384–322 BCE) countered with *eudaimonia*, a calmer, kinder, more nourishing form of pleasure: a sense of purpose, connectedness, contentedness.

Laozi is a contemplative, a meditator, and a finder of calm. Because he lives simply, the world opens up to him, and he can find beauty in the simplest things. He does not need to rush around seeking exotic pleasures. He has learned that contentment in simple things can deliver a more fulfilling happiness than the vicissitudes of life lived in the fast lane. He has rejected the hedonic pleasures of Aristippus and embraced Aristotle's *eudaimonia*. Laozi is right, of course, but I wonder how appropriate it is to advocate calm and contented living for young people. Surely it is okay for people in their late teens and early twenties to raise some hell. It might be valuable—or even necessary.

My own life has slowed down in a way that I have found deeply rewarding—and this has been unexpected. If asked at twenty-nine how I would feel about the prospect of slowing down at fifty-nine, I would probably have expressed dismay. The twenty-nine-year-old me would not have relished the idea of a future of bumbling about a modest house taking pleasure in the decidedly slow-paced pleasures of reading, writing, painting, and working with wood. But I am much happier and more relaxed than I was back then. The twenty-nine-year-old me was a bit of a wreck, manic, always pushing for more. I was unsatisfied with my life for decades. In truth, I was unsatisfied with myself. Don't get me wrong. I have never been an unhappy person, and my manic life has been quite normal, but I have spent most of it forging onward, restlessly. Is it madness, all this push-push-push? Perhaps it is, but it was also good to me. I wonder if I would have found today's calm had I not lived some measure of yesterday's storm.

So, there may be no rush. Living according to your nature might mean that in youth you should live a more energetic, hormone-driven existence in which *passing pleasures* have a legitimate place. But eventually and in your time you will find that Laozi was right. You can *let the world come to you. It will come quietly and peacefully.* There will be a time for this, and it is available when you are ready. Indeed, as unenticing as it may look from the vantage point of youthful busyness, because *the Path boasts no exotic flavors, no dramatic vistas, no grand music,* it turns out that *you can never have too much of it.* My new hedonism is a comfy chair in a quiet corner, a nice glass of wine (okay, maybe two), and a good book.

VERSE 36. THE WEAK ARE STRONGER

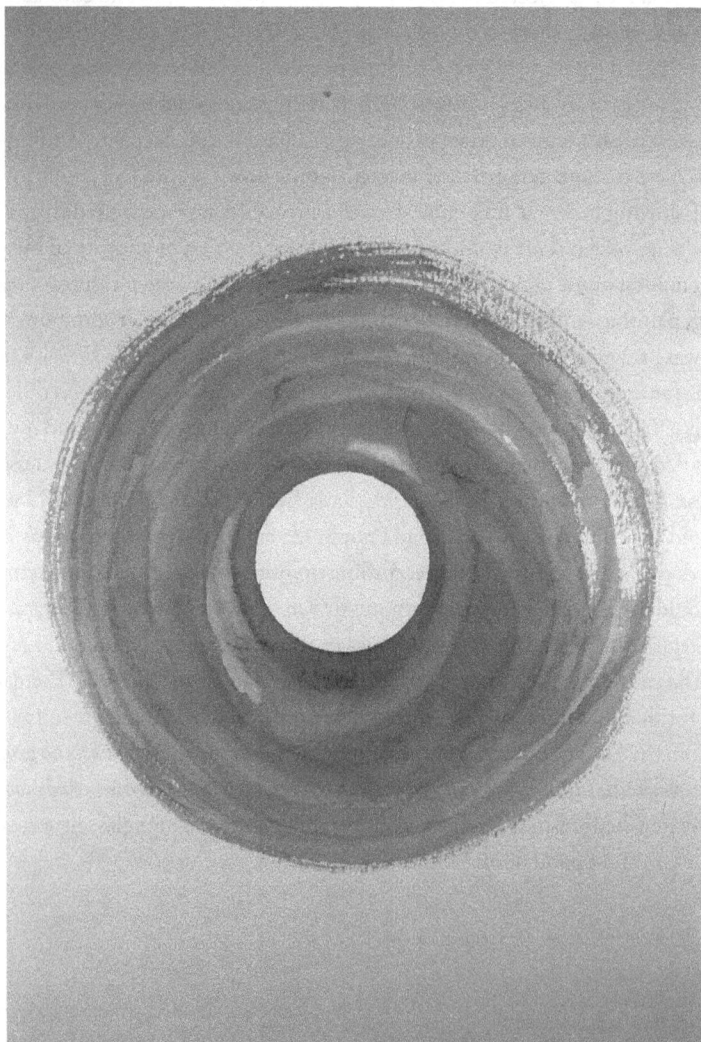

Glazed enso donut

36 三十六

jiāng yù shè zhī bì gù zhāng zhī 将 欲 歙 之 必 固 张 之

jiāng yù ruò zhī bì gù jiàng zhī 将 欲 弱 之 必 固 强 之

jiāng yù fèi zhī bì gù xīng zhī 将 欲 废 之 必 固 兴 之

jiāng yù qǔ zhī bì gù yú zhī 将 欲 取 之 必 固 与 之

shì wèi wēi míng 是 谓 微 明

róu ruò shèng gāng qiáng 柔 弱 胜 刚 强

yú bù kě tuō yú yuān 鱼 不 可 脱 于 渊

guó zhī lì qì bù kě yǐ shì rén 国 之 利 器 不 可 以 示 人

To draw something in
  first stretch it out
To make something weak
  first allow it to grow strong
For a thing to be ruined
  it must first be raised
For a thing to be seized
  it must first be given

This is the secret insight
  how the soft and weak
  defeat the hard and strong

The big fish that rises up from the deeps
  can be hooked
The country that brandishes all its weapons
  can be overthrown

We return to the Dao's emphasis on yin over yang. The weak are stronger: *This is the secret insight, how the soft and weak defeat the hard and strong.* Laozi likes to use water as a metaphor, and my mind always goes first to the image of water flowing gently over limestone, eroding it into a cave, water dripping from stalactites that stretch down from a domed ceiling, stalagmites reaching up as if designed to catch the droplets, and the cave walls sculpted into lace curtains.

Laozi explains how to use the yin-yang polarity to overcome brute force by exploiting its brittleness. Strong things may lack suppleness. Robust things may lack resilience. If you bend metal, it will eventually fatigue. If you stretch glass, it will shatter. Yang strength is like stone. It holds its form perfectly until it fails, but when it does fail, it fails hugely. Yin strength is like rubber. It loses its form easily but returns to it quickly. To defeat yang-style strength, *first stretch it out* and *allow it to grow strong.*

The most famous victory of yin over yang is the story of David and Goliath (1 Samuel 17). The small, young, casually clad Judean shepherd scampered down into the valley of Elah with his sling to face the huge, armored, Philistine warrior, Goliath of Gath. This dude was huge: "six cubits and a span"! The staff of his spear was "like a weaver's beam"! His coat of mail was "five thousand shekels of brass"! It was a total mismatch—but not in the way we are told. Goliath never had a chance. Shepherding is not for the fainthearted, and David was highly trained. He could kill lions and bears with that slingshot of his. The cumbersome, overburdened, weighed-down yang Goliath was no match for the nimble yin David.

The most expansive archetype for the enduring strength of weak things is DNA. A planet devoid of life was transformed into one replete with it. How? Stable chunks of chemistry evolved into forms that replicated themselves. The replicators came into competition with each other, and those who collected (ate) their building blocks more effectively thrived, as did those who figured out how to eat other replicators, avoid being eaten, assumed a more complex physical structure (legs, perhaps, or eyes); learned to parasitize, avoid being parasitized, or grew wings; camouflaged themselves, grew teeth, or a big brain with a large prefrontal cortex, and so on.

DNA is not a strong, hard molecule. Leave some out on the lab bench, and it will degrade in minutes, be consumed, and vanish. And yet its softness—its yin—belies an incredible capacity for endurance. It has survived for the better part of four billion years, since that first serendipitous replication in the primordial soup. It is weak, soft, supple, and yet it is more forever than diamonds and stronger than granite. It represents the ultimate strength of flow. It is Earth come to life.

VERSE 37. *WUWEI* FOR THE MIND

Great Sand Dunes National Park, Colorado

37   三十七

dào cháng wú wéi ér wú bù wéi	道常无为而无为
hóu wáng ruò néng shǒu zhī	侯王若能守之
wán wù jiāng zì huā	万物将自化
huā ér yù zuò	化而欲作
wú jiāng zhèn zhī yǐ wú míng zhī pǔ	吾将镇之以无名之朴
wú míng zhī pǔ fū yì jiāng wú yù	无名之朴夫亦将无欲
bù yú yǐ jìng tiān xià jiāng zì dìng	不欲以静天下将自定

The Path maintains eternal nonaction
and yet leaves nothing undone

If leaders could abide by its example
everything would transform naturally

If desires were to arise
they would be calmed
The nameless uncarved block tempers desire

With desire managed all is quiet
The world settles into peace

The last verse of the first book of the *Daodejing* offers a clean, simple summary of some of the main themes so far: *wuwei*, the *uncarved block*, and the attenuation of *desires*.

First, we are reminded that the Dao is all-powerful and animates the cosmos effortlessly. It *maintains eternal nonaction and yet leaves nothing undone.* The Dao operates by doing not-doing, by not meddling, by acting through inaction, by effortless action performed in a state of uninhibited excellence, by *wuwei*.

Second, we bring this observation of the natural world into the human world. If leaders could follow the example of the Dao, argues Laozi, everything would simply fall into place. This has been one of the key themes of the first part of the *Daodejing*. We should resist the urge to control. Nothing in nature needs to be controlled. Little in life is improved when it is controlled.

Third, we are reminded to temper our desires. This has been another frequent theme of the *Daodejing*. Cravings and ambitions are not healthy ways to seek happiness; they are stresses that inflict unnecessary suffering. Consider the uncarved block, perfect and untrammeled in its uncarved state. Leave your mind like that. The mind that craves is unhappy and leaves us in a state of mental discomfort. Meditation, quietness, and calm train the mind to resist unnecessary craving.

Finally, we are reminded that the uncarved block is the most honest and direct path to happiness. It represents simplicity, nonstriving, and infinite possibility. The great sculpture is revealed from the uncarved block by stripping away superfluous material. Nature is the uncarved block. It is never more beautiful than when left untouched. We are the uncarved block. We are never more perfect than when we are simple, honest, and uncontrived.

So, we take the uncarved block and admire it. We see the beauty within it but avoid meddling with it or wanting to shape it to our needs. It cannot be improved, so we let it be. Slow down. Do less. Control your cravings. Desire is managed. *All is quiet. The world settles into peace.*

VERSE 38. A GREAT SECOND BEST

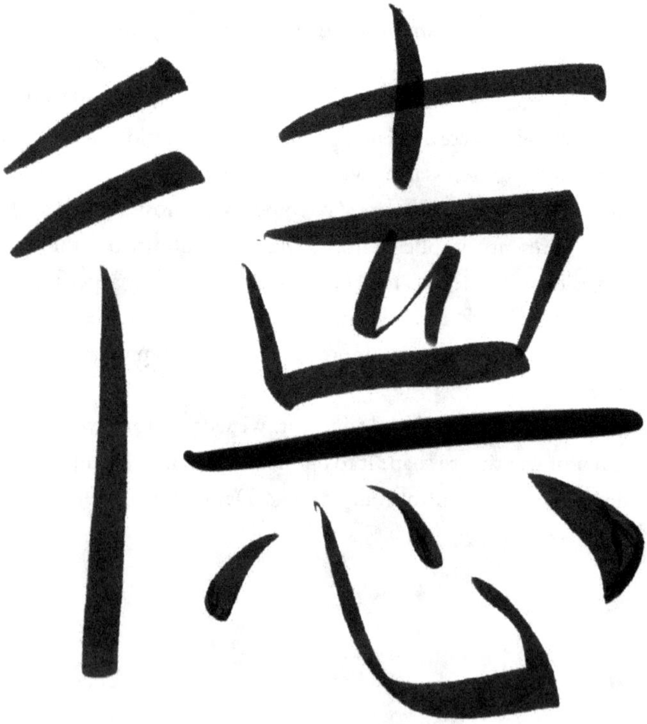

De character: Virtue, etc.

38 三十八

shàng dé bù dé shì yǐ yǒu dé	上德不德是以有德
xià dé bù shī dé shì yǐ wú dé	下德不失德是以无德
shàng dé wú wéi ér wú yǐ wéi	上德无为而无以为
xià dé wú wéi ér yǒu yǐ wéi	下德无为而有以为
shàng rén wéi zhī ér wú yǐ wéi	上仁为之而无以为
shàng yì wéi zhī ér yǒu yǐ wéi	上义为之而有以为
shàng lǐ wéi zhī ér mò zhī yǐ yìng	上礼为之而莫之以应
zé rǎng bì ér rēng zhī	则攘臂而扔之
gù shī dào ér hòu dé	故失道而后德
shī dé ér hòu rén	失德而后仁
shī rén ér hòu yì	失仁而后义
shī yì ér hòu lǐ	失义而后礼
fū lǐ zhě zhōng xìn zhī báo ér luàn zhī shǒu	夫礼者忠信之薄而乱之首
qián shí zhě dào zhī huá ér yú zhī shǐ	前识者道之华而愚之始
shì yǐ dà zhàng fū chǔ qí hòu bù jū qí báo	是以大丈夫处其厚不居其薄
chǔ qí shí bù jū qí huá	处其实不居其华
gù qù bǐ qǔ cǐ	故去彼取此

True virtue is higher than virtue   unassuming
    and therefore virtuous
Fake virtue is simply for display
    and therefore not virtuous at all

The most virtuous observe nonaction
    and are unselfish
The less virtuous make sure they are seen to act
The kind act generously
The righteous act ostentatiously
Those who follow the rules blindly earn no respect
    and so they roll up their sleeves
    and act with force

Lacking Dao we fall back on De
Lacking De we fall back on kindness
Lacking kindness we resort to morality
Lacking morals we resort to rituals and rules

Rituals may have the appearance of loyalty and honesty
    but they reside at the edge of chaos
Blind obedience to the rules
    is the fountainhead of stupid

The wise reside in the core
    not on the surface
    in the fruit   not the flower

They reject that
and accept this

The *Daodejing* is usually separated into two books, with verses 1–37 representing Book 1, sometimes called the Dao Book, and verses 38–81 representing Book 2, sometimes called the De Book, although the division based on content is far from clear. This first verse of the second book does, however, offer a proper introduction to De.

De can be interpreted a number of ways. I tend to translate it as "virtue," but it can also be translated as "bounty," "power," "to be grateful," and in other ways depending on context. In this verse, I leave it untranslated in the third stanza. The Chinese character for De is compounded from three characters: to walk, to look ahead, and the heart-mind (*xin*). So, virtue: to walk honestly while looking ahead. My choice of the word "virtue" does not come without some risk. The word has been tainted by prudish uses, but I have no interest in "virtuous maidens" and the like. I interpret the virtue represented by De as a strictly good and honest characteristic completely free of puritanical or prudish smear. De is, of course, the second character in *Daodejing* (*Dao De Jing*). It is the ultimate practical expression of the Dao, but it is strictly second best. De is not Dao. (*Jing* simply means "classic," as in "text of.")

Laozi seems to use the first half of this verse to tidy up his own understanding of De as meaning human virtue. Any action that attempts to spotlight one's own virtue is immediately disqualifying—egotism tarnishes virtue, and such virtue lacks depth. True virtue is modest and characterized by *wuwei*. Truly virtuous people act with compassion and humility, whatever the circumstances. They do not act in order to be seen to act.

We are all familiar with the "look at me being all virtuous 'n' all!" behavior: virtue-signaling by using the right branded products; making sure to be seen giving to charity; generously donating to your alma mater, virtuously, but making sure it names a building after you. It is all such obvious egotism. Give aid, offer help, be kind, and expect nothing in return. This is virtue.

Laozi is no lover of rituals and false morals. (It is amazing, then, that a religion sprang from his words.) His hierarchy of praiseworthy behavior is very clear: Dao over De, De over kindness, kindness over morality, and morality over rituals and rules. Rituals *have the appearance of loyalty and honesty but they reside at the edge of chaos. Blind obedience to the rules is the fountainhead of stupid.* These societal norms and values are only necessary if kindness is not enough, and nor is kindness the ultimate virtue; only De can be that. And the only thing superior to De is Dao.

True virtue comes not from ambitions, achievements, or desires fulfilled but instead from deep within. *It resides in the core, not on the surface; in the fruit, not the flower.* Virtue has nothing to do with outward beauty, skill, or charm. It has everything to do with core values, right action, and the relinquishment of control. The virtuous reject the flashy, obvious glamour of the flower. They look deeper, to heart of things: to the fruit.

VERSE 39. EVERYTHING IS LINKED

Stork

39	三十九
xi zhi de yi zhe	昔之得一者
tian de yi yi qing	天得一以清
di de yi yi zhu	地得一以宁
shen de yi yi ling	神得一以灵
gu de yi yi ying	谷得一以盈
wan wu de yi yi sheng	万物得一以生
hou wang de yi yi wei tian xia zhen	侯王得一以为天下贞
qi zhi zhi	其致之
tian wu yi qing jiang kong lie	天无以清将恐裂
di wu yi zhu jiang kong fei	地无以宁将恐废
shen wu yi ling jiang kong xie	神无以灵将恐歇
gu wu yi ying jiang kong jie	谷无以盈将恐竭
wan wu wu yi sheng jiang kong mie	万物无以生将恐灭
hou wang wu yi zhen jiang kong jue	侯王无以贞将恐蹶
gu gui yi jian wei ben	故贵以贱为本
gao yi xia wei ji	高以下为基
shi yi hou wang zi cheng gu gua bu gu	是以侯王自称孤寡不谷
ci fei yi jian wei ben xie	此非以贱为本邪
fei hu	非乎
zhi yu wu yu	至誉无誉
bu yu lu lu ru yu	不欲琭琭如玉
luo luo ru shi	珞珞如石

These ancient things attained wholeness

The sky   which became clear
The earth   which became placid
The spirits   which became divine
The valley   which was filled
The ten thousand things   which were brought to life
The kings of old   who were virtuous

If the sky loses its clarity   it might shatter
If the earth loses its tranquility   it might splinter
If the spirits lose their divinity   they might dissipate
If the valley is not replenished   it will empty and dry up
If the ten thousand things are not nurtured they might be annihilated
If the ruler is not virtuous   he will fall

Noble has its origins in the common
The foundation of high is low

This is why rulers claim to be orphans   widows   beggars
They know the lowly are the root of the exalted

Don't desire to be precious like jade
Be tough like common stone

Some verses of the *Daodejing* have an insanely contemporary feel to them. When was this verse written? Two and a half thousand years ago? That doesn't seem possible. Surely it was written in the last few decades by some environmentally conscious poet. Surely it is about climate change, species extinctions, pollution, and the depletion of soil and water resources. *If the sky loses its clarity it might shatter. If the valley is not replenished it will empty and dry up.*

The population of the planet was probably only two hundred million or so when this was written: a fiftieth of today's. There were no plastics and no fossil fuels. Complex civilizations had emerged in many parts of the world, including China, but they were separated by cultural and geographic boundaries. Much of humanity lived in small nomadic, hunter-gatherer, and mixed emergent agrarian societies. It is hard to imagine that anyone could have had an ecological conception of the planet as a connected entity, and yet here we are: hard to imagine only for a lack of imagination. This is an environmental warning for the modern world passed down from the ancient one.

In my discussion of verse 32 I speculated that it would be fun to bring Laozi to the modern world to show him the physics of the cosmos. I imagine he would also be impressed with many other things: art, music, movies, photography. There is great beauty in the modern world, but I fear he would be aghast at what he would see in the natural world. We live in a world much impoverished since the time of Laozi. The sky *has* lost its clarity. The earth *is* far from tranquil. Many valleys *do* run dry.

How have we managed to do so much damage to the world? Central is our tendency to desire too much, to want more than we need. We move from one moment of progress to the next, always wanting more and always feeling justified that we should expect more. This is true even for environmentalists. How many flights are flown to environmental conferences? How many papers are published? How many careers are made? How many new technologies are urgently needed, urgently developed, and urgently deployed?

Everything is linked: predator to prey, forest to soil, land to ocean. And the ecological world is linked to the economic world. If people and corporations can amass a pool of capital, they can use that to spend down a pool of natural resources: an aquifer, a forest, an ocean of fish. And the economic world is linked to the mental world. What people and communities consume is linked to how they see themselves and their society. And so, the environment is linked to the human mind. We crave to *be precious like jade.* The solution is to see the beauty in being *tough like common stone.*

VERSE 40. EVERYTHING IS CYCLIC, EXCEPT EVERYTHING

Skein of geese over Celery Bog Nature Area, West Lafayette, Indiana

40 四十

fǎn zhě dào zhī dòng 反者道之动

ruò zhě dào zhī yòng 弱者道之用

tiān xià wàn wù shēng yú yǒu 天下万物生于有

yǒu shēng yú wú 有生于无

The motion of the Path is circular
The method of the Path is yielding

Everything is born of being
except being
which is born of nothing

A microbe dies in a compost pile. It is quickly consumed by its cousins, who produce more microbes who will consume them in their turn. The cycles of birth, gorging, and death are so frenetic that the compost pile heats up. It swarms with life, steaming, until its jumble of dead leaves, stems, twigs, and scraps has become a sponge of plant food. Scooped up and spaded into the garden, it propels the luxuriant growth of turnips, cabbages, and tomatoes that will give nutrients and energy to human bodies that will gorge and die in their turn. All energy and all nutrients are but borrowed, and eventually you will have to give them back.

Fog clasps my cold window, condenses, worms its way down the pane, drips onto the pavement, gathers into a culvert and then a stream and finds its way to the river. From the river to the sea. From the sea deep into the ocean following some vast current that draws it across to another continent. Flowing to the surface, now evaporating, now rising as vapor, blown over the land, cooling, condensing into a thick fog that clasps your window ten thousand miles away.

Or consider a molecule of carbon dioxide that once diffused through the stomatal pore of some grand ancient lycopod. Fixed as glucose, shuffled to the trunk, glued in as cellulose or lignin serving to hold the giant tree upright, lifting its leaves to the sun. Then falling, but not decaying: stuck, anoxic, squashed, crushed, pressurized deep underground. Left to pyrolyze for half a billion years. Then mined and burned in a power plant and released back into the atmosphere at a most inconvenient time.

A supernova explodes. A thin cloud of gas splatters out into the vastness of space and coalesces, laggardly, into a nebula. The nebula crashes together over billions of years— a slow-motion star wreck!—to form new suns.

Everything is cyclic. Everything is born from something else. Matter is organized into one form, disorganized, and reorganized into another. Energy makes the organizations. The disorganizations make energy. *Everything is born of being except being.*

What began before everything began? Well, I have no idea. *Being was born of nothing,* says Laozi, but I don't know what that means.

VERSE 41. STUDENTS OF THE PATH

White roses

41 四十一

shàng shì wén dào qín ér xíng zhī	上 士 闻 道 勤 而 行 之
zhōng shì wén dào ruò kún ruò wáng	中 士 闻 道 若 存 若 亡
xià shì wén dào dà xiào zhī	下 士 闻 道 大 笑 之
bù xiào bù zú yǐ wéi dào	不 笑 不 足 以 为 道
gù jiàn yán yǒu zhī	故 建 言 有 之
míng dào ruò mèi	明 道 若 昧
jìn dào ruò tuì	进 道 若 退
yí dào ruò lèi	夷 道 若 纇
shàng dé ruò gǔ	上 德 若 谷
dà bái ruò rǔ	大 白 若 辱
guǎng dé ruò bù zú	广 德 若 不 足
jiàn dé ruò tōu	建 德 若 渝
zhì zhēn ruò yú	质 真 若 渝
dà fāng wú yú	大 方 无 隅
dà qì wǎn chéng	大 器 晚 成
dà yīn xī shēng	大 音 希 声
dà xiàng wú xíng	大 象 无 形
dào yǐn wú míng	道 隐 无 名
fū wéi dào shàn dài qiě chéng	夫 唯 道 善 贷 且 成

When the best student hears of the Path
she studies in order to follow it
When the average student hears of the Path
her understanding comes and goes
When the weakest student hears of the Path
she laughs out loud
    but then   without laughter
    it wouldn't be the true Path

So it is said
The brightest Path appears dark
Advancing along the Path seems like retreating
The level Path is rugged
The most elevated virtue is a valley
The clearest things are opaque
The most abundant virtue feels insufficient
The staunchest virtue seems unsteady
The purest thing seems tainted

The great square has no corners
The perfect tool is unfinished
The finest music is hushed
The greatest image is blurred

The Path is hidden and nameless
yet only the Path gives and completes

Advancing along the Path seems like retreating. The level Path is rugged, and *the most abundant virtue seems insufficient*. This Path, discovered through the Dao, might not be straight or straightforward. It is not a sequence of things to learn, as learning is conventionally understood. It is not characterized by the acquisition of knowledge. It is more like unlearning.

What we find along the path might be troubling. Things that looked right now look wrong. *The purest thing seems tainted*, and *the greatest image is blurred*. Our perception of the world changes, and not all the changes are expected or desired. We begin to notice and be moved by things that once passed us by. It all sounds like quite serious business.

And perhaps it is serious business. People have often laughed at the innovations that showed us new ways of thinking. Charles Darwin was laughed off the stage. Descendants of monkeys? Ludicrous! Galileo was laughed into house arrest. Circling the sun? Preposterous!

But I don't think that's the right interpretation here. Here's a thing: I think Laozi uses this verse to take a swipe at pretentious students of the Dao. The first stanza seems like a hierarchy from best student to good to worst, as we might expect. It seems as though he's lauding the best student—the person who *studies in order to follow* the Path—and that he is satisfied with the average student for whom *understanding comes and goes* and is disappointed with the weakest student who, when she *hears of the Path, she laughs out loud*. The correct interpretation, I believe, is that Laozi sees the laughter of the "weakest" student as natural and honest. The one who studies seriously is contrived and much too pleased with herself. The giggling student is the most natural person in the room—and therefore the most in harmony with the Dao.

And who wouldn't laugh out loud at a moment of enlightenment? Aha!

Shakespeare's fools tend to be the wisest characters in his plays. In *Twelfth Night*, for example, Feste, the fool, is the only person with a license to tell the truth: "Better a witty fool than a foolish wit." In *As You Like It*, Touchstone, the fool, might be the only self-aware character in the play: "The fool doth think he's wise, but the wise man knows himself to be a fool."

Laozi repeatedly tells us that the path is wide. He repeatedly tells us to be modest and humble. He also tells us that wisdom is superior to knowledge. Why would he advise us to be overly studious and serious? The Dao isn't that complicated. Be happy. Be kind. Is all.

VERSE 42. DAO, QI, MODESTY, AND A SIMPLE RULE

Bamboo

42   四 十 二

dào shēng yī	道 生 一
yī shēng èr	一 生 二
èr shēng sān	二 生 三
sān shēng wàn wù	三 生 万 物
wàn wù fù yīn ér bào yáng	万 物 负 阴 而 抱 阳
chōng qì yǐ wéi hé	冲 气 以 为 和
rén zhī suǒ ě wéi gū guǎ bù gǔ	人 之 所 恶 唯 孤 寡 不 谷
ér wáng gōng yǐ wéi chèn	而 王 公 以 为 称
gù wù huò sǔn zhī ér yì	故 物 或 损 之 而 益
huò yì zhī ér sǔn	或 益 之 而 损
rén zhī suǒ jiāo wǒ yì jiāo zhī	人 之 所 教 我 亦 教 之
qiáng liáng zhě bù dé qí sǐ	强 梁 者 不 得 其 死
wú jiāng yǐ wéi jiāo fù fù	吾 将 以 为 教 父 甫

Dao birthed one
One birthed two
The two birthed a third
The three birthed the ten thousand things

The ten thousand things carry
    yin on their backs and enfold
    yang in their arms
They blend with their Qi to attain harmony

++++

People loathe being abandoned   alone   unworthy
which is perhaps why kings take these as titles

Gain can come from losing
Loss can be the result of gaining

So here is a simple rule
The violent die violent deaths
This is a good basis for teaching

The *Daodejing* was not written in eighty-one verses but instead as a single, undivided document, as we saw in verse 23. It was divided into eighty-one verses at some later date because the number nine holds special significance in Daojiao, and therefore 9 x 9 = 81 gives the document added numerical mystique. Sure, okay, but verse 42 obviously addresses at least two distinct themes, arguably three.

First, the Dao and the Qi. Ursula Le Guin, in her beautiful translation of the *Daodejing*, calls this section a "pocket cosmology," and I really like that phrase. The Dao is the originator. It gives rise to the opposing-complementary forces of yin and yang, of which all things are made. Yin and yang give rise to the three treasures or three jewels: *jing*, or essence; *shen*, or spirit; and Qi, or breath. The Qi, the breath, or vital breath, breathes life into the ten thousand things, which is to say all living things. Exactly how all this works is a mystery. "And God said, 'Let there be light!' And there was light." That works too, as does the Lenape creation myth in which Kishelamakank creates life through the four Spirit Beings and as does the Hindu cosmology of Brahma and Shiva, the creator and the destroyer of worlds. Nobody knows what came "first." Choose something and knock yourself out. To Laozi, it is the mysterious, all-encompassing Dao.

Second, modesty and a simple rule. We meet this unexpected explanation of kings calling themselves *abandoned, alone, unworthy* in the first two lines. Was this the case in Laozi's time? It seems unlikely that we would hear modern politicians canvasing people for votes by calling themselves these things. Leadership in the modern world does not seem to select for such self-effacing types, and I'm not entirely convinced it ever did. Wishful thinking, perhaps? The next two lines jump into a new theme: *gain can come from losing* and *loss can be the result of gaining*, which is a common power inversion of the *Daodejing*. The idea is a common one in the latter part of the *Daodejing*, where Laozi frequently advises leaders to act with humility and lead with restraint. Leaders who align with the masses and gain their support gain power.

The final stanza points to what might happen to those who reject the restrained path and opt for the violent one. *The violent die violent deaths.* That's clear enough. "Those who live by the sword die by the sword" (Matthew 26:52).

VERSE 43. BE LIKE WATER, LIKE AIR

Village in Guangxi, China

43　四十三

tiān xià zhī zhí róu	天下之至柔
chí chēng tiān xià zhī zhí jiān	驰骋无下之至坚
wú yǒu rù wú jiàn	无有入无闻
wú shì yǐ zhī wú wéi zhī yǒu yì	吾是以知无为之有益
bù yán zhī jiāo	不言之教
wú wéi zhī yì	无为之益
tiān xià xī jí zhī	天下希及之

The softest things in the world
    override the hardest
The formless
    infiltrate the impenetrable

Thus we understand the influence
    of doing not-doing
    of teaching without telling

Few possess this influence

One of the overarching themes of the *Daodejing* is the idea that people should follow their nature and that they can understand their nature by observing and following nature writ large. Force gives the appearance of superiority when small achievements are overblown, and short time frames are mistaken as long. People see great significance in a battle between two armies, but a battle is a skirmish amid the longer forces of civilizations. People live and die. Kings, cities, and empires rise and fall. And the entire history of humans is but a blink of nature's eye. Even with climate change, the great human-caused disaster of our time, nature will adjust and flow on. Our time, like all things, this too will pass.

The softest... override the hard seems like a reference to water, and *the formless infiltrate the impenetrable* seems like a reference to air. Their power is subtle and slow but unrelenting. People are animated by water and air. They dry up when they stop breathing. Buildings, cities, and even mountains are eroded away by the tireless scorings and scuffings of the wind and the rain. Water and air are the archetypes of a remorseless yin force that acts with the ultimate patient and persistent *wuwei*. *Thus we understand the influence of doing not-doing.*

Laozi then adds the idea of *teaching without telling*, which advances the concept of *wuwei* one step further. To learn *wuwei* from nature is to learn its patience and gentle persistence. The next step is to learn how to pass that along to others, to teach with the gentle persistence of nature, to *teach without telling*. This instruction is reminiscent of the frequent diktat of creative writing teachers: show, don't tell. Overtelling a story can strip it of its vitality. Certain things must be gently revealed or sparingly shown so the story is felt rather than explained.

People can learn a lot from teachers who tell them things: blue light has a shorter wavelength than red light, elephants are bigger than echidnas, water freezes and ice melts, $2 + 2 = 4$. Got it. This is the basic concept of knowledge transfer, Teaching 101, but learning beyond knowledge is a different matter. Learning to analyze and synthesize information and learning to develop one's own self-awareness and ethics are much less straightforward. These wisdoms are beyond the realm of simple teaching by telling. They must be shown, and sometimes they can only be pointed at. Teaching and learning such things aren't easy. This is where we begin to cross from the basic realm of knowledge toward the advanced realm of wisdom. It takes the patience of water and the gentle persistence of air.

VERSE 44. ENOUGH IS ENOUGH

Purdue Student Farm, West Lafayette, Indiana

44 四十四

míng yú shēn shú qīn	名 与 身 孰 亲
shēn yú huò shú duō	身 与 货 孰 多
dé yú wáng shú bìng	得 与 亡 孰 病
shì gù shén ài bì dà fèi	是 故 甚 爱 必 大 费
duō cáng bì hòu wáng	多 藏 必 厚 亡
zhī zú bù rǔ	知 足 不 辱
zhī zhǐ bù dài	知 止 不 殆
kě yǐ cháng jiǔ	可 以 长 久

Which matters more
    your name or your body?
Which is more precious
    your body or your wealth?
Which is more painful
    loss or gain?

Great desire can be costly
Hoarded wealth can be lost

Know when you have enough
    there's no disgrace in that
Know when to stop
    there's no danger in that

The key to lifelong contentment

Fame, wealth, ambition, and lust each present a significant danger to our mental health, and Laozi admonishes us to know when enough is enough. This theme is central to numerous religions and philosophies.

Jesus of Nazareth, recently baptized in the River Jordan, wandered into the Judean wilderness, where he fasted for forty days and was tempted by Satan. Jesus refused Satan and returned to Galilee to begin his ministry. "The true servants of the Most Compassionate are those who walk on the earth humbly, and when the foolish address them improperly, they only respond with peace" (Quran, sura Al-Furan 63). Prince Siddhartha Gotama had been closeted away in the palace, protected from the ills of the world, but eventually came to understand that the world was full of suffering. He escaped the palace and wandered, penniless, for years on a quest to find the meaning of life. Finally, starving, he sat for days in contemplation beneath the Bodhi tree, did battle with Mara, his mind-demons, and came to understand that physical suffering was just a small part of the suffering of people and that the larger part was in their minds. Through this awakening Siddhartha found the Middle Way and became the Buddha.

These stories of the hero archetype reveal a universal human struggle. We are all engaged in a great struggle with our own minds whether we are aware of it or not. Our minds are not our own unless we make them so. They belong, as Dan Harris explains in his book *10% Happier,* to the "asshole in our head."[18] We must wrest control of our minds from this asshole. Meanwhile, we are also all aware of the moments of transcendence of which the mind is capable. These can manifest as feelings of wonderful expansiveness, as a sense of being in communion with something much larger than ourselves. It is pretty damn cool, and we tend to experience it when our mind is running on autopilot, when it gets out of its own way, when the mind finds a state of "flow." Meditation can open up such states, as can painting or riding a motorcycle. I see no reason why prayer or gymnastics—or tiddlywinks, I suppose—shouldn't have similar effects. Part of the irony of human arrogance is that we assume that our own way of reaching transcendence is the only way, but how would we know that's not just the asshole in our heads talking?

There are a thousand ways to find enlightenment, but all the great philosophies agree that one necessary condition is to tamp down the desires and control the cravings. And maybe some mythical enlightenment may remain out of reach, but if you *know when you have enough* and *when to stop,* you will have found *the key to lifelong contentment.*

VERSE 45. STILLNESS OVERCOMES HEAT

Happy Hollow Park, West Lafayette, Indiana

45　四十五

dà chéng ruò quē qí yòng bù bì	大成若缺其用不弊
dà yíng ruò chōng qí yòng bù qióng	大盈若冲其用不穷
dà zhí ruò qú	大直若屈
dà qiǎo ruò zhuó	大巧若拙
dà biàn ruò nè	大辩若讷
jìng shèng zào	静胜躁
hán shèng rè	寒胜热
qīng jìng wéi tiān xià zhēng	清静为天下正

The great whole seems incomplete
    but can be used forever
The completely full seems empty
    but can never be drained

The straightest seem curved
Great skill appears clumsy
The most eloquent seem to mumble

Movement overcomes cold
Stillness overcomes heat
Calmness keeps the world in order

Let's start with the remarkable observation that *stillness overcomes heat*. It is as wonderful as the line *who, by nothing but stillness, can render muddy water clear?* (v. 15). These are the ultimate expressions of *wuwei* for an era of escalating climate crisis. We now know that human impacts on the climate were already beginning in ancient China as a consequence of the expansion of rice cultivation and animal husbandry, but Laozi could have had no inkling of this, and yet *stillness overcomes heat* remains our only real solution to the climate crisis.

Most of the solutions we want to deploy to mitigate climate change involve some kind of action—urgent action, immediate action, desperate action—but action generates heat. *Movement overcomes cold.* We need more efficient cars so we can drive just as fast, just as far, while burning less gasoline, we are told. We need more efficient agriculture so we can produce more food more quickly to feed more mouths using less water and fertilizer, we are told. But more technology that can do more things more efficiently neither calms nor cools. Our focus should be on slowing down and doing less. We know this, but it seems so hard.

Even worse are the desperate geoengineering schemes that have been concocted to cool the planet by blasting sulfur dust or tiny mirrors into the atmosphere, by fertilizing the oceans to create explosive growths of algae, or by particle-seeding clouds. The ultratechnologists would have us cool the planet by reengineering nature so we could move as fast as we wanted, generate as much heat as we wanted, and air-condition Earth. No. Stop this madness.

Impossible, you say? But the world is huge, and its resources are vast. *The great whole can be used forever. The completely full seems empty but can never be drained.* Jan Baptiste van Helmont performed the definitive experiment demonstrating earth's productivity in the 1630s. He weighed dry soil into a pot and then added a willow sapling and began to water it. Five years later the willow had grown into a 169-pound tree, and the soil had lost only an ounce of weight. Remarkable: plants are made mostly from water and air! You'd think we'd be able to stay within nature's insanely generous limits. All the resources we need—not all the ones we want, mind you, but all the ones we need—are renewable. When we slow down—or are slowed down—they will renew.

Movement generates heat—*movement overcomes cold.* If you want to reduce heat, to cool down, you must slow down and do less—*stillness overcomes heat.*

VERSE 46. THE CURSE OF CRAVING

Akureyri, Iceland

46　四十六

tiān xià yǒu dào	天 下 有 道
què zǒu mǎ yǐ fèn	却 走 马 以 粪
tiān xià wú dào	天 下 无 道
róng mǎ shēng yú jiāo	戎 马 生 于 郊
huò mò dà yú bù zhī zú	祸 莫 大 于 不 知 足
jiù mò dà yú yù dé	咎 莫 大 于 欲 得
gù zhī zú zhī zú cháng zú yǐ	故 知 足 之 足 常 足 矣

When the world is on the Path
fine stallions leave their manure in the fields
When the world loses its Way
mares are bred for warhorses

The greatest mistake is desire
The worst misfortune is discontent
The greatest curse is craving

When you are content with enough
There is always enough

The last couplet of this verse completes the theme begun in verse 44 by stating, quite simply, that *when you are content with enough there is always enough*. Sufficiency is less a function of how much you have than how much you need. The way to be content with moderation and sufficiency is to manage *desire, discontent*, and *craving*. Simple enough? Simple to understand, yes, but not so simple to implement.

Happiness is the best thing there is, and the most precious gift one person can give to another (and themself). The problem is not happiness but rather the *pursuit* of happiness. (I know, I know, it is right there in the second sentence of the Declaration of Independence.) Achieving a goal gives us a burst of happiness, but it is fleeting. We soon drop back to our prior state. Neither great successes nor great failures affect our happiness in the ways we expect. We predict that we will be forever happy when we win the lottery, perform to a sell-out crowd at Madison Square Garden, or become CEO of a company, but when we achieve these lofty ambitions, we soon sink back toward our previous baseline state. Actually, we can sink lower. The disastrous lives of lottery winners are legion. The opposite adaptation also happens. We expect that we would be shattered if we were to lose our job, say, or be seriously injured in an accident. Again, we adapt. We rise back toward our baseline state surprisingly quickly. Be thankful. Enough is enough. Count your blessings. Yes, the cloying truisms here are true.

My favorite part of this verse, however, is the first stanza. I love the way Laozi uses horses as a vehicle of metaphor for conflict and peace that links the state of society, the state of our minds, the state of our farms, and the state of the environment. When war breaks out there is a desperate call to action. Everything becomes urgent, nothing is productive, and everything is rushed. Even mares are pressed into service. During times of peace, we may get the chance to slow down. Even the fine stallions can find peace on the farm, leaving their manure in the fields. Laozi conjures a lovely bucolic scene. Everything is slower, more thoughtful, and well tilled and fertilized.

The way we treat our animals is an indicator of how we treat our environment and ourselves. When the world loses its way, animals are commodified, raised in concentrated animal feeding operations, killed en masse in high throughput slaughterhouses, and divvied up in packinghouses. Even the products derived from this high throughput slaughter—the cheap, processed fast-food fatty beef patty drive-throughs—are symptoms of a tortured world.

VERSE 47. SEE WITH OTHER EYES

Old Town Square, Prague, Czechia

47　四十七

bù chū hù zhī tiān xià　不 出 户 知 天 下

bù kuī yǒu jiàn tiān dào　不 窥 牖 见 天 道

qí chū mí yuǎn qí zhī mí shǎo　其 出 弥 远 其 知 弥 少

shì yǐ shèng rén bù xíng ér zhī　是 以 圣 人 不 行 而 知

bù jiàn ér míng　不 见 而 明

bù wéi ér chéng　不 为 而 成

Know the world
    without leaving your front door
Know heaven's Path
    without looking out of the window

The further you go the less you know

The wise know without going out
They see without looking
They don't act   and yet they complete

Jane Marple and Hercule Poirot are two of Agatha Christie's most memorable characters, and both are genius detectives. Poirot is a sophisticated, worldly, well-traveled, snappy-dressing Belgian gentleman with a waxed pointy mustache. His genius comes from a huge breadth of experiences gained through a cosmopolitan life. Jane Marple is rather dowdy and has hardly ever left her little English village of St. Mary Mead, and yet she is every bit Poirot's match. Her genius comes from careful observation and a deep knowledge of place. If a blade of grass is askew on the village cricket pitch, she can deduce that Auntie Elsie's godson has stolen a teacup from the vicarage.

You might say that Monsieur Poirot is a yang detective and Miss Marple is a yin one, and I think Laozi would have been a big fan of Miss Marple. She *knows the world without leaving her front door* and exemplifies the contention that *the further you go the less you know*.

I love to travel, and travel has been a huge part of my personal development. I feel the need to defend travel and find common ground with Mark Twain here, who said that "travel is fatal to prejudice and bigotry," but I think there's ample common ground between Mark Twain and Laozi. The point is how and why we travel and with what mental luggage. If a Chinese tourist visits Disneyland, has she really visited America? An American tourist visiting China should taste hot pot in Leshan as well as sweet and sour chicken at one of those nasty high-throughput tourist restaurants beside the Great Wall at Badaling. And if you treat travel as an escape from your life, your return is likely to be a disappointment. Be sure to take yourself fully on the trip. In any case, Laozi did not have tourism in mind here. What worried him was people who looked outside the village to escape to a better life. He cautions us that the grass is not always greener on the other side of the fence and that the best path to green grass might be to tend your own lawn.

This verse is also a metaphor for the mind. When Laozi tells us that we can *know the world without leaving your front door*, he's also telling us that we can know ourselves without leaving our own heads. When he tells us that we can *know heaven's path without looking out of the window*, he's also referring to the window of our eyes. We can see without looking by introspection and meditation. Going out into the world means taking your "self" out into the world—but you have no self. You are not a self. *The wise know* this *without going out*. Some people will find happiness in a new place, but most of us carry our state of mind with us wherever we end up. Or, as Marcel Proust said in *In Search of Lost Time*, "The only true voyage of discovery, the only fountain of Eternal Youth, would be not to visit strange lands, but to see with other eyes." So, whether a traveler or not, explore the landscape between your ears. You can take that with you wherever you go.

VERSE 48. GAIN
THE WORLD

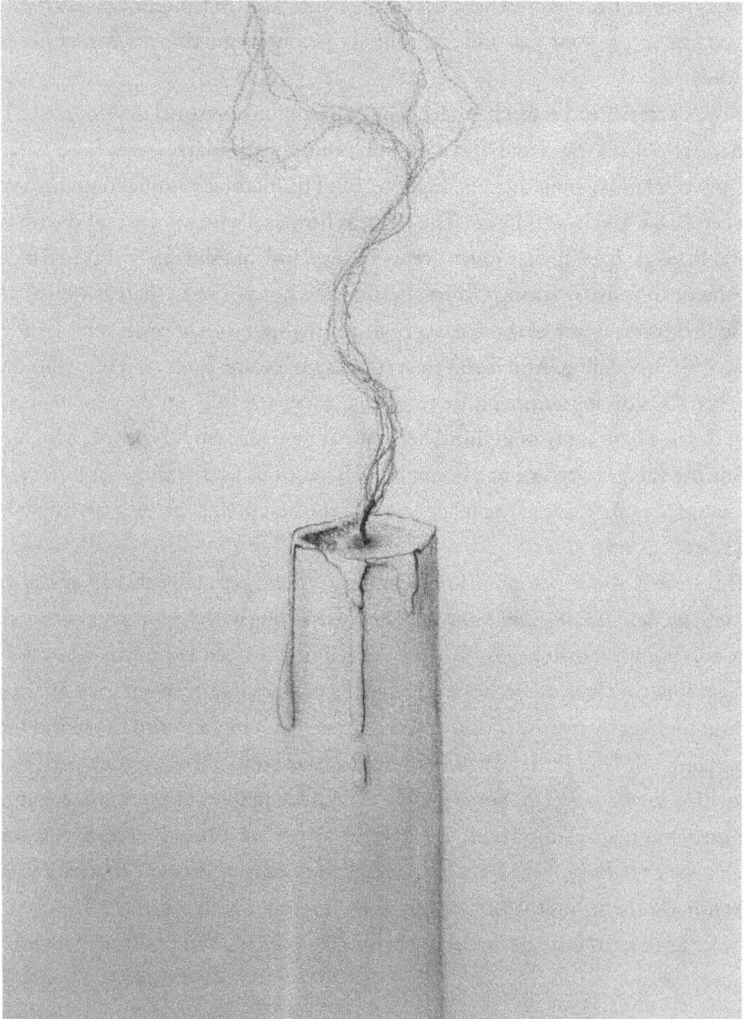

Candle

48　四十八

wéi xué rì yì	为 学 日 益
wéi dào rì sǔn	为 道 日 损
sǔn zhī yòu sǔn	损 之 又 损
yǐ zhì yú wú wéi	以 至 于 无 为
wú wéi ér bù wéi	无 为 而 不 为
qǔ tiān xià cháng yǐ wú shì	取 天 下 常 以 无 事
jí qí yǒu shì	及 其 有 事
bù zú yǐ qǔ tiān xià	不 足 以 取 天 下

Those who study daily
    gain knowledge daily
Those who practice Dao daily
    relinquish knowledge daily
    dwindling until they master not-doing

Not-doing
    to ensure that nothing is left undone

Gain the world by not-doing
Try to control the world
    and it will evade you

Surely Laozi is not suggesting that we abandon learning when he says *Those who practice Dao daily relinquish knowledge daily*? This verse appears to present us with a paradox, but the paradox is resolved by a deeper understanding of *wuwei*. Laozi is not warning us away from all learning and knowledge; he is warning us about cleverness, or craftiness, and he is particularly concerned about the use of knowledge for control. *Those who practice... and relinquish... dwindle until they master not-doing*. Again, this is the strange idea of doing not-doing. Why would that require practice? Well, because it goes against our nature and against our culture. Ceding control is hard.

Practice is always about doing. You practice tennis by hitting tennis shots, practice archery by loosing arrows, and practice the piano by playing scales and arpeggios. If you want to get better at something, you practice it. Practice doesn't make perfect; practice makes permanent. (Practicing badly will reinforce bad habits.) This ancient wisdom has been given a mechanism by modern science. The Buddha said, "Whatever a person frequently thinks and reflects on becomes the pattern of their mind," and then, more than two thousand years later, neuroscientist Donald Hebb said, "Neurons that fire together wire together."[19] Disused neural networks weaken, while those that are exercised strengthen. Weirdly, you can (only slightly) improve those tennis shots, bull's-eyes, and scales and arpeggios by playing them over in your mind. So, if we want to master not-doing, we need to practice it. The practice for learning to not-do is to do a whole lot of not-doing. In meditation, train the mind to resist reactivity and find equanimity. And then do it again. And then again.

So, what can you gain by not-doing? The verse reminds us that *wuwei* is not found in knowing to control, but rather in knowing not to control. *Wuwei* is the patience to let things be. The knowledge that enables us to see that clever fixes are often not so clever. Some systems, especially natural systems, are best left alone. Force the land to produce mountains of corn in vast monocultures, and you will grapple for control with fertilizers and pesticides, soil health will degrade, pests will evolve resistance, and control will become harder and harder. What's more, the agricultural system that controls and controls to produce and produce will shape a food system with a million unhealthy corn chips, corn nuts, corn puffs, corn flakes, corn pips, and corn syrups. You'll find that you've invested billions into food and farming systems that cause environmental degradation and diabetes.

The *wuwei* sustainability message is spelled out in the last lines of the verse: *Try to control the world and it will evade you*. Not only will the world evade our attempts to control it, but when we embrace the world with not-doing, that's when we find it. *Gain the world by not-doing*.

VERSE 49. SIMPLE KINDNESS

Lotus

49 四十九

shèng rén wú cháng xīn	圣 人 无 常 心
yǐ bǎi xìng xīn wéi xīn	以 百 姓 心 为 心
shàn zhě wú shàn zhī	善 者 吾 善 之
bù shàn zhě wú yì shàn zhī dé shàn	不 善 者 吾 亦 善 之 德 善
xìn zhě wú xìn zhī	信 者 吾 信 之
bù xìn zhě wú yì xìn zhī dé xìn	不 信 者 吾 亦 信 之 德 信
shèng rén zài tiān xià shè shè yān	圣 人 在 天 下 歙 歙 焉
wéi tiān xià hún qí xīn	为 天 下 浑 其 心
bǎi xìng jiē zhù qí ér mù	百 姓 皆 注 其 耳 目
shèng rén jiē hái zhī	圣 人 皆 孩 之

The wise have no preconceived ideas
so they embrace the needs of the people

They treat good people well
and they treat bad people well
Thus they have the virtue of goodness

They are trusting of people who are honest
and also of those who are dishonest
Thus they have the virtue of faithfulness

The wise engage with the world
and remain simple at heart
Thus the people turn their eyes to them
and their childhood is restored

The wise described in this verse appear to have either childlike naivety or superhuman restraint. *They treat bad people well. They are trusting of those who are dishonest.* We assume that the wise know that people can be bad and dishonest but treat them well and with trust nonetheless.

There is a common archetype revealed here, and one of its most famous avatars is Jesus of Nazareth. John (8:7) says that Jesus protected the adulteress by standing with her and defying the mob, saying "Let him who is without sin cast the first stone," and that Jesus trusted Judas Iscariot even though he knew Judas would betray him in the Garden of Gethsemane (6:64). The life of Jesus of Nazareth has been deeply dishonored by people with many different ideas and ideals. Modern America's ghastly Christian nationalists, for example, appear to worship a selfish, vindictive, capitalist Jesus who has nothing in common with the ideals taught in either the Bible or the *Daodejing*. The Jesus described by his brother James and some of Jesus's disciples appears to have been an honest man of the people and a hero of nonviolent resistance and finds common ground here. The power of simple kindness in a violent world made Jesus of Nazareth and Laozi true radicals—exemplars of radical, unilateral kindness—and kindred spirits.

The final stanza opens with these simple words: *The wise engage with the world and remain simple at heart.* This describes a challenge that is far from simple. One can imagine remaining simple at heart by withdrawing from the world, being distracted from it, or by ignoring its constant commotions. One can imagine retreating to a wilderness outpost and becoming simple at heart by avoiding the frustrations of dealing with people. Get away from it all. We all imagine that from time to time as a means of coping with bad people and dishonest people—or just people some days. But that's not what the wise lauded in this verse do. Laozi's wise engage. They accept the world's madness and clamor and its random acts of unfairness, pain, and misery. They let it all in, and yet they still remain simple at heart. Just as common sense is not so common, simple kindness is not so simple.

And just a quick comment about the closing lines. When the wise have performed their magic of coping with clamor while remaining engaged and simple at heart, the stanza says that *their childhood is restored.* Why their childhood? This is another theme of the *Daodejing*, the recognition of the simple, honest purity of the child—specifically the child's mind, which has yet to be contaminated by the complex machinations of adult desires and cravings. The name "Laozi," after all, can be translated as "old master" or "old child."

VERSE 50. HOW TO LIVE

Addis Ababa, Ethiopia

50   五十

chū shēng rù sǐ	出生入死	
shēng zhī tú shí yǒu sān	生之徒十有三	
sǐ zhī tú shí yǒu sān	死之徒十有三	
rén zhī shēng dòng zhī yú sǐ dì	人之生动之于死地	
yì shí yǒu sān	亦十有三	
fū hé gù	夫何故	
yǐ qí shēng shēng zhī hòu	以其生生之厚	
gài wén shàn shè shēng zhě	盖闻善摄生者	
liù xíng bù yù xiōng hǔ	陆行不遇凶虎	
rù jūn bù bèi jiǎ bīng	入军不被甲兵	
xiōng wú suǒ tóu qí jiǎo	凶无所投其角	
hǔ wú suǒ yòng qí zhuǎ	虎无所用其爪	
bīng wú suǒ róng qí rèn	兵无所谷其刃	
fū hé gù	夫何故	
yǐ qí wú sǐ dì	以其无死地	

Between birth and death
    three in ten pursue life
    three in ten pursue death
    three in ten rush toward death
by pursuing their desires

Only the tenth
    can walk on the hills
    without meeting wild buffalo or tiger
    can enter a battle
    without weapons or armor

The buffalo finds no place to jab its horn
The tiger finds no place to sink its claws
The soldier finds no place to thrust his knife

Why?
The tenth one
    does not present a place for death

Three in ten pursue life. This probably refers to people who survive to old age but never fully live, gain wisdom, or attain enlightenment.

Three in ten pursue death. This statistic is fairly consistent with perinatal and infant mortality rates throughout much of human history.

Three in ten rush toward death by pursuing their desires. This probably refers to those killed violently by rushing into hotheaded fights, seeking glory in war, or untimely deaths from things such as addiction and suicide.

Only the tenth. Precious few, a tenth of us, lives wisely and fully. These superheroes are immune to wild animal attacks and invulnerable in battle.

No, not literally. This verse is probably one of the reasons Daoism got all tangled up with strange ideas about immortality. Daoism can protect you from tigers in the mountains and knives on the battlefield? Cool, I'll have me some of that! But no, it is obviously metaphorical. (And no, Noah didn't actually put two of every animal on a big boat, and no, Jonah didn't actually spend a weekend in the belly of a big fish, and no Allah didn't split the moon in two, and no the Buddha doesn't come back to life after death in the body of some cute child from Qinghai.) The buffalo, which can find *no place to jab his horn*, the tiger, which can find *no place to sink its claws*, and the soldier, who can find *no place to thrust his knife* are metaphorical assaults on the mind by desires and cravings, the forces of yang arrayed against yin, and the demands to defeat dominate, and control. The wise prepare their minds to give these assaults no place.

But what about that one-in-ten statistic? When Laozi speaks of *only the tenth* he's speaking of only ten percent of the population, but ten percent of billions is a lot. Are there really hundreds of millions of wise people in the world? That's a lot of wise people. What's your reaction to this? Mine was "No way! There are nowhere near that many enlightened people!" And I also wondered, "Am I one of them?" Everyone's above average, right? But would you dare to live life walking in the tiger-infested hills or to enter battle unarmed and without armor?

VERSE 51. THE PRIMAL DE

In the hills above Dharamsala, India

51　五十一

dào shēng zhī dé chù zhī	道 生 之 德 畜 之
wù xíng zhī shì chéng zhī	物 形 之 势 成 之
shì yǐ wàn wù mò bù zūn dào ér guì dé	是 以 万 物 莫 不 尊 道 两 贵 德
dào zhī zūn dé zhī guì	道 之 尊 德 之 贵
fū mò zhī mìng ér cháng zì rán	夫 莫 之 命 而 常 自 然
gù dào shēng zhī dé chù zhī	故 道 生 之 德 畜 之
cháng zhī yù zhī	长 之 育 之
tíng zhī dú zhī	亭 之 毒 之
yǎng zhī fù zhī	养 之 覆 之
shēng ér bù yǒu	生 而 不 有
wéi ér bù shì	为 而 不 恃
cháng ér bù zǎi	长 而 不 宰
shì wèi xuán dé	是 谓 玄 德

Dao gives birth to them
De raises them
Matter forms them
Energy animates them

and each of the ten thousand things
respects Dao and honors De

Their respect for Dao
and honor for De
are not by command
but by virtue of their very being

Because Dao gives them life
And De raises them
    nurtures them
    teaches them
    shelters and heals them
    protects and comforts them

To raise without possessing
To nourish without spoiling
To guide without controlling

This is the Primal De

De is the Great second best to the Dao (v. 38), and I tend to translate De as Virtue, although its meaning, like that of Dao, is hard to pin down. Here, a more active definition of De might be warranted, such as "power" or "motivating force," and as Laozi lists the various roles of De and the ways the world responds to De, we begin to understand its power and reach. Laozi also introduces the concept of Primal De in this verse, and it seems to represent the pinnacle of De to the point that De becomes almost synonymous with Dao.

This verse opens with another "pocket cosmology," to repeat the phrase from Ursula Le Guin (v. 42). *Dao gives birth to them; De raises them; matter forms them; energy animates them.* The Dao and the De, then, are forces more fundamental than matter and energy: something beyond physics, something supernatural. Laozi seems to be trying to wrap his head around things that are really too big and complex to fully realize in the imagination. We know there's stuff, and we know that energy is required to make it go, but what actually sets everything in motion? Well, that problem won't get resolved here, but once things are in motion, the wide-ranging responsibilities of De will become clear. De will be tasked with almost every aspect of the lives of the ten thousand things.

Dao remains more fundamental than De in this verse but seems to assign most of the work to De. The ten thousand things (i.e., all of life) are raised, nurtured, taught, sheltered, healed, protected, and comforted by De. A hefty workload like that sounds a lot like a traditional framing of the work of a mother, some form of Earth Mother, perhaps, who does all of this in the most self-effacing way. She makes everything perfect and then let's go, neither possessing, spoiling, nor controlling. *This is the Primal De.*

God genders are interesting. If you're going to invent a god, you can go with a boy god, a girl god, or a nonbinary god. If you're polytheistic you can mix it up. The ancient Egyptians invented Ra, Isis, and Hapi. The ancient Greeks invented Zeus, Aphrodite, and Hermaphroditus. Many indigenous societies worship female, yin-power gods, often referred to as Earth Mothers. The Inca Pachamama watched over the work of planting and tending crops and supervised the harvest. Unci Maka is Grandmother Earth to the Lakota people. In Haudenosaunee mythology, Sky Woman, Atahensic, falls to Earth through a hole in the sky onto the back of a giant turtle. There are many iterations of Earth Mother among Indigenous Australians, including the Sun Mother, who is central to many Australian creation myths.

The monotheistic religions are different. If you are to have only one god, what gender will you choose? Well, as it turns out, male. Of particular note is the masculine yang-power god of the world's dominant invader-colonizer culture. Europe invaded the world with an all-powerful, all-conquering, all-loving, etc. male god. How much can the global crises we face today be linked to the yang ethic of our cultures?

VERSE 52. SEAL
THE OPENINGS

Coneflower and butterfly

52　五十二

tiān xià yǒu shǐ yǐ wéi tiān xià mǔ　天下有始以为天下母

jì dé qí mǔ yǐ zhī qí zǐ　既得其母以知其子

jì zhī qí zǐ fù shǒu qí mǔ　既知其子复守其母

méi shēn bù dài　没身不殆

sāi qí duì bì qí mén zhōng shēn bù qín　塞其兑闭其门终身不勤

kāi qí duì jì qí shì zhōng shēn bù jiù　开其兑济其事终身不救

jiàn qí xiǎo yuē míng shǒu róu yuē jiàng　见其小曰明守柔曰强

yòng qí guāng fù guī qí míng wú yí shēn yāng　用其光复归其明无遗身殃

shì wéi xí cháng　是为习常

In the beginning was the mother of the world
Knowing her you can know her children
    and the children can return you to the mother
    free of sorrow

Seal the openings   close the doors
and life will always be easy
Succumb to the desires of the outer world
and you will suffer to the end of your days

To see the small is enlightenment
To remain tender is strength
Use its light
    to return to clarity
    avoid misery
    and learn constancy

We continue to consider the Earth Mother in a second verse that has layers within layers. It touches on many of the themes of the *Daodejing*, and yet its touch is so deft that its meanings are simultaneously profound and easily missed—a complexity only possible in poetry. Knowing the *mother of the world* you can *know her children*, and they can *return you to the mother free of sorrow*. Death holds no fear for those who know the mother of the world, the Dao itself, in feminine, yin, form. Your place in the grand scheme of things is small. You are born. You return. This kind of thing happens a lot.

The middle stanza offers some practical advice. *Succumb to the desires of the outer world and you will suffer to the end of your days*. Yikes. Sounds bad. And how should we avoid this tragedy? *Life will always be easy*, says Laozi, if you *seal the openings* and *close the doors*. This could mean a few different things.

Laozi can be a bit saucy at times, and I think he intends us to cast our nasty little minds to the openings of the body. Succumbing to the desires? Sealing your openings might be a good idea, madame, monsieur. The most obvious desires are sexual but also gustatory, in which case sealing the openings and closing the doors is a good idea to limit your gluttony. The deeper meaning of sealing the openings and closing the doors, however, is to manage the trivial but constant desires and cravings of the mind and to maintain inner peace. The reference, then, is to mental openings and doors, and if there's one particularly unhealthy thing to which humans are addicted and that tends to go unnoticed, it is the addiction to unskillful and unmindful thoughts. *Seal the openings* and *close the doors* to shut out the addictive thoughts that mess with the mind.

The third stanza layers the teaching that enlightenment comes from seeing the perfection in small, simple things and from having the tenderness and the capacity to yield. As he so often does, Laozi points us toward yin and asks us to consider the strength of tenderness. Initially, the Dao is the light that shows the path that leads away from misery and toward clarity. You are a speck floating down a huge river—a terrifying image until you let go and engage with the wonder of being part of a big beautiful river.

So, verse 52 is a road map. First, understand the context of impermanence. Second, learn to close to the doors to cravings and desires. Third, be wary of yang and open to yin in order to find balance. You will then be able to *return to clarity, avoid misery, and learn constancy*.

VERSE 53. LEAD US NOT INTO TEMPTATION

The Singing Window at the Tuskegee University Chapel, Tuskegee, Alabama

53 五十三

shǐ wǒ jiè rán yǒu zhī 　使 我 介 然 有 知

xíng yú dà dào wéi shī shì wèi 　行 于 大 道 唯 施 是 畏

dà dào shén yí ér rén hǎo jìng 　大 道 甚 夷 而 人 好 径

cháo shén chú tián shén wú cāng shén xū 　朝 甚 除 田 甚 芜 仓 甚 虚

fú wén cǎi dài lì jiàn 　服 文 彩 带 利 剑

yàn yǐn shí cái huò yǒu yú 　厌 饮 食 财 货 有 余

shì wèi dào kuā 　是 谓 盗 夸

fēi dào yě zāi 　非 道 也 哉

It only takes the least scrap of sense
to stay on the broad Path
but I fear wandering off

The broad Path is flat and straight
but people are fond of detours

The palace is full of splendor
 while the fields are choked with weeds
 and the granaries are left bare
They dress in extravagant clothes
 sporting fine swords at their side
 gorging on exotic food and drink
 accumulating wealth in abundance

This boastfulness and vanity is robbery
by people who have most certainly left the Path

道　　盗

Dao: Dao, Way, Path　　Dao: Theft, Robbery

Ursula Le Guin has the plainest of footnotes beneath her translation of this verse. It simply says "So much for capitalism." Nice. This verse uses a lovely play on words, exploiting the fact that *dao* is a near-homophone, one meaning of which is "path, way, or road," which we have seen frequently, and the other meaning of which is "robbery." The penultimate line is *this boastfulness and vanity is robbery* (*dao*), and the final line is *by people who have most certainly left the Path* (Dao).

Laozi's special targets in this verse are greedy officials who are not doing their job to protect the people. Food security has been a key governmental role for millennia. The story of Joseph in Genesis 41 portrays the development of ancient Egypt's first granaries. The history was embedded in a story about the Pharaoh's dreams of seven years of plenty (fat cows and fat sheaves of grain) to be followed by seven years of famine (emaciated cattle and withered crops) that offered a biblical account of ancient Egyptian agricultural policy. Here, Laozi tells us that *the fields are choked with weeds and the granaries are left bare*. Meanwhile, what's going on at the palace, at the center of government? It is *full of splendor*, and its denizens are dressed *in extravagant clothes*, with *fine swords at their side*, while *gorging on exotic food*. They are using their positions of power to enrich themselves. They are *dao*: robbers.

This verse is direct and straightforward. Officials who use their positions to advance themselves while people below them in the social hierarchy suffer and while the work they should be doing for others is left undone have left the path. This is particularly frustrating because *it only takes the least scrap of sense to stay on the broad Path*.

This verse can be read two ways, I think. In one reading, I sense a frustrated Laozi railing against selfish and incompetent governance. *The Path is flat and straight*, and so the fact that these charlatan bureaucrats are leaving the fields choked with weeds and leaving the granaries bare while they live high on the hog exposes them as robbers. This reading is certainly part of the intention of this verse, but I sense a second message. Laozi is also self-aware and concerned that his own darker tendencies may lurk beneath the surface. He too must guard against selfishness and abuse of privilege. Other people have clearly strayed from the path, and he knows that *it only takes the least scrap of sense to stay on the broad Path, but I fear wandering off*.

VERSE 54. THINK GLOBALLY, ACT LOCALLY

Farmworkers in rapeseed field, Dehradun, India

54　五十四

shàn jiàn zhě bù bá	善建者不拔
shàn bào zhě bù tuō	善抱者不脱
zǐ sūn yǐ jì sì bù chuò	子孙以祭祀不辍
xiū zhī yú shēn qí dé nǎi zhēn	修之于身其德乃真
xiū zhī yú jiā qí dé nǎi yú	修之于家其德乃余
xiū zhī yú xiāng qí dé nǎi cháng	修之于乡其德乃长
xiū zhī yú bāng qí dé nǎi fēng	修之于邦其德乃丰
xiū zhī yú tiān xià qí dé nǎi pǔ	修之于天下其德乃普
yǐ shēn guān shēn	以身观身
yǐ jiā guān jiā	以家观家
yǐ xiāng guān xiāng	以乡观乡
yǐ bāng guān bāng	以邦观邦
yǐ tiān xià guān tiān xià	以天下观天下
wú hé yǐ zhī tiān xià rán zāi	吾何以知天下然哉
yǐ cǐ	以此

What is well rooted is not easily pulled
What is firmly attached is not easily separated
Your descendants will honor their ancestors for generations

Cultivate yourself to develop genuine virtue
Cultivate your family to foster a wealth of virtue
Cultivate the village to support enduring virtue
Cultivate the country to promote abundant virtue
Cultivate the world to sustain universal virtue

Therefore
In myself I see the self
In my family I see what family means
In my village I see all villages
In my country I understand what countries are
In the world I see everything under heaven

We begin with botanical images. An important goal is to be well rooted and firmly attached. The benefits of this will be persistent: they will be passed down through the generations. Next, cultivating (another plant propagation image) should be done by yourself, your family, your village, your country, and your world—in that order. The hierarchy links your local actions to global consequences. As an aside, this sense of hierarchy is more characteristic of Kongzi (Confucius) than Laozi. Daoism is in many ways a philosophical objection to the strict ritualization of rules and morals found in Confucianism, but the two philosophies do have linked origins.

There is an array of higher-order problems that require coordinated responses. Global climate change requires us to reduce carbon emissions and increase carbon sequestration, and there are many practical ways to do this, but we are unable to coordinate action among competing corporations and countries. And each corporation and country's rationale is that "if I do this but they don't, I'll be outcompeted." There are many global problems of this kind. If we don't scoop up ocean fish, someone else will. If we don't use wood from old-growth forests, someone else will. If we don't exploit cheap labor, cheap resources, and cheap land in the Global South, someone else will. If we don't drill oil wells, someone else will.

Laozi gives a practical answer to the person who feels hopeless in the face of modern global crises. What can a single individual do—especially a regular prole like me who lacks wealth, power, and position? You can take care of yourself and serve altruistically at the level at which you operate. We too often wash our hands of higher-order issues by saying "I don't have the power to fix this," but relinquishing authority and embracing powerlessness can catalyze its own self-fulfilling prophecy.

One such self-fulfilling prophecy is the tragedy of the commons. When a shared resource faces degradation, who should act? Everyone should act, of course, but if people feel disconnected, the result can be tragedy. The classic scenario is a pasture where several independent villagers graze their sheep. The pasture is degrading from overgrazing. What to do? Well, shepherds must reduce their flocks, of course, but if a villager doesn't trust his neighbors to reduce their flocks, he is unlikely to reduce his. The solution is to cultivate your own virtue and to cultivate the virtue of the village by helping to build trust. So-called commoners actually do have a strong history of managing the commons effectively because people can form trusting, cohesive communities. It is actually countries and corporations that act out their selfishness on the commons. They do not build trust. The tragedy of the commons should be renamed the tragedy of the corporations.

So, in answer to the question "But what can I do, little old me?," the answer is that you can cultivate what you can even if it is only yourself. Don't be the accelerant that turns a spark into a wildfire. Be the firebreak that checks communal selfishness. And advocate and vote for any and all policies that limit the freedoms of corporations on the commons.

VERSE 55. RETURN TO INFANCY

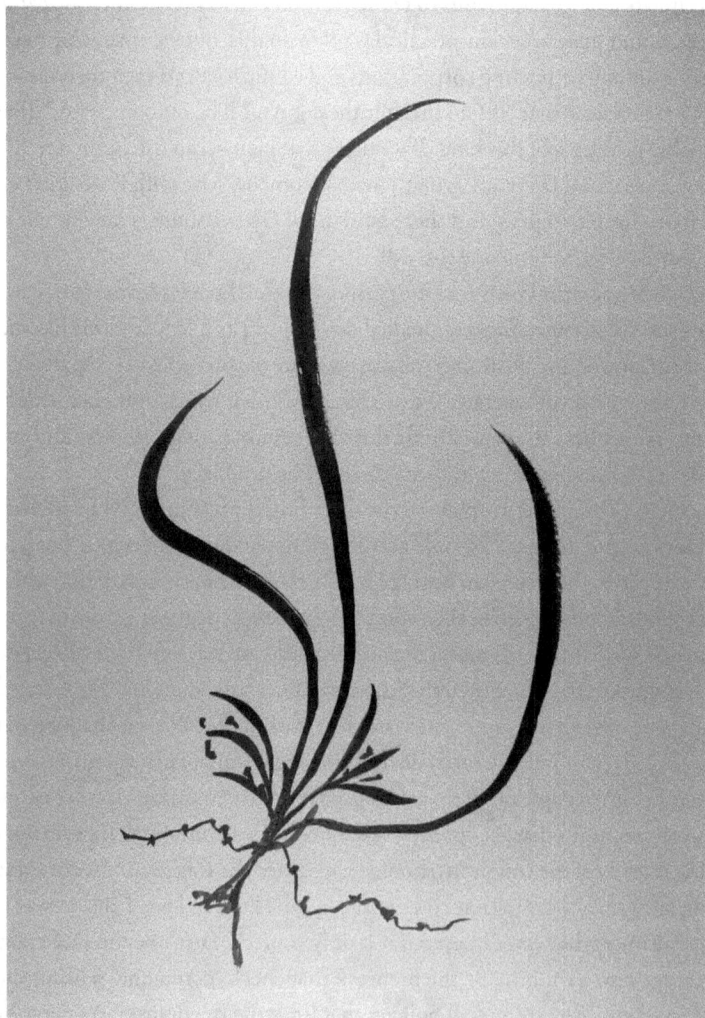

Orchid seedling

55 五十五

hán dé zhī hòu bǐ yú chì zǐ	含德之厚比于赤子
dú chóng bù shì	毒虫不螫
měng shòu bù jū	猛兽不据
jué niǎo bù tuán	攫鸟不抟
gǔ ruò jīn róu ér wò gù	骨弱筋柔而握固
wèi zhī pìn mǔ zhī gě ér quán zuò	未知牝牡之合而全作
jīng zhī zhì yě	精之至也
zhōng rì háo ér bù á	终日号而不嗄
hé zhī zhì yě	知之至也
zhī hé yuē cháng	知和曰常
zhī cháng yuē míng	知常曰明
yì shēng yuē xiáng	益生曰祥
xīn shǐ qì yuē jiàng	心使气曰强
wù zhuàng zé lǎo wèi zhī bù dào	物壮则老谓之不道
bù dào zǎo yǐ	不道早已

To fully embody virtue
be like a newborn
Venomous insects   scorpions   snakes
will not bite or sting him
Wild animals will not claw him
Birds of prey will not swoop down on him

His bones are weak
his muscles are tender
and yet his grip is tight

He has yet to experience sex
and yet he gets firm erections
His vitality is great!

He screams and cries all day
without getting hoarse
His harmony is true!

To know this harmony is to know the eternal
To know the eternal is to be enlightened

Overfilling life is foolish
Letting the mind control the Qi is perilous

It causes exhaustion   a turning from the Path
What turns from the Path soon ends

The third stanza gives me such a laugh. I'm smiling as I write, imagining my two grown boys cringing as I tell the world "Yes, they not only peed little fountains when their parents were trying to change their diapers but also got little stiffies." And yes, all my kids could've screamed for gold at the Olympics, and yes, even when they were barely days old they had a grip like a pipe wrench. I'm not sure about the mystical protection against predators—seems risky. I always figured it was my job to make sure that never got tested.

The return to infancy—specifically the return to simplicity, innocence, and unobstructed pure thought—is a common theme in the *Daodejing*. The advice is in stark contrast to most advice: Stop acting like a child! Grow up! Act like a man! It couldn't be made clearer than in 1 Corinthians 13:1: "When I was a child I spake as a child, I understood as a child, I thought as a child: but when I became a man I put away childish things." And it is not just impatient saints and parents who want to hurry children swiftly into adulthood. The desire also eventually afflicts children, and this is a terrible shame, but children do become restless to grow up. They don't want to be kids anymore. They want to be adults, and they can suffer great feelings of inadequacy. It is a deep-seated example of the "I will be happy when . . ." problem; a failure to live in the now, an early example of craving causing mental suffering.

The stresses of work seem modern: bullshit jobs,[20] office politics, working overtime, being put on another project when you already have too much to do. These stresses are often self-inflicted for the sake of status and prestige, but *overfilling life is foolish*. It can cause terrible stress over things that assume false importance in our minds. *Letting the mind control the Qi is perilous. It causes exhaustion.*

Laozi lauds the short period of mental bliss that we enjoy when all we have to do is be. We just have to follow a simple path. We don't feel that there's anything wrong with us. We look like we should look, and we know the things we should know. We have no fear of death. We are learning rapidly, but we haven't yet figured out that we should stress out if we don't learn fast enough. The venomous insets, scorpions, and snakes and the claws of the wild animals and birds of prey allude to mental assaults. Fully developed minds devise all manner of self-torture: doubts, anxieties, and, of course, cravings and desires. One way to master the afflictions of the adult mind is to be like a child: to try to recapture some of the bliss of living with a child's mind. Life was easier when we were children and can be easier again if we can recover some measure of the clarity of the carefree childhood mind.

VERSE 56. CLOSE
THE DOORS

Organoponico Vivero in Alamar, Cuba

56 五十六

zhī zhě bù yán yán zhě bù zhī	知者不言言者不知
sāi qí duì bì qí mén	塞其兑闭其门
cuò qí ruì jiě qí fēn	挫其锐解其纷
hé qí guāng tóng qí chén	和其光同其尘
shì wèi xuán tóng gù	是谓玄同故
bù kě dé ér qīn	不可得而亲
bù kě dé ér shū	不可得而疏
bù kě dé ér lì	不可得而利
bù kě dé ér hài	不可得而害
bù kě dé ér guì	不可得而贵
bù kě dé ér jiàn	不可得而贱
gù wéi tiān xià guì	故为天下贵

Those who know don't speak
Those who speak don't know

Subdue your senses   Constrain your desires
Blunt your sharpness   Unravel your knots
Soften your glare

Be as dust
A profound unity

Those who attain this cannot be
    seduced or rejected
    promoted or impeded
    honored or disgraced

Therefore they are the most highly revered

Some of the lines in this verse are almost identical to lines in verse 52 where Laozi advised us to *seal the openings* and *close the doors*, and the message here is the same: seek integrity and self control. The first stanza reminds us that Laozi is not a fan of blowhards. *Those who know don't speak. Those who speak don't know.* This reminds me of the Abe Lincoln quote: "Better to remain silent and be thought a fool than to speak and remove all doubt."

The second stanza covers the practical advice already seen in verse 52. Find your happy place through simplicity. Be serene and under control. Control your desires and cravings. I also like the phrases *blunt your sharpness* and *soften your glare.* Be patient with people. Try not to snap at them.

Then, we are advised, *Be as dust. A profound unity.* What an enigmatic phrase. I love that. What, exactly, does he mean? I presume that Laozi is speaking of dust in the same way we use the phrase "earth to earth, ashes to ashes, dust to dust" at funerals. He is speaking of real dust, the fine, dry particles of soil back into which life is returned after death. *Be as dust.* Be like the soil, the Earth. *A profound unity.* Be one with the earth. Be of the earth.

With our desires and cravings under control and having found our unity with the earth, we are invincible. *Those who attain this cannot be seduced or rejected.* Relationships are conducted on our own terms. Neither can we be *promoted or impeded.* Our position in life will be of our own choosing. We will never again beg for a pay raise or fear being fired. Finally, we can no longer be *honored or disgraced.* We are what we are, and other people's views of us is their business, not ours.

This verse encapsulates the first three of the Buddha's Four Noble Truths. The First Noble Truth is the existence of daily mental suffering: *dukkha.* The Second Noble Truth is that *dukkha* arises from cravings and desires: *tanha.* The Third Noble Truth is that *tanha* can cease, preventing *dukkha,* leading us to *nirvana.* The Fourth Noble Truth expounds the Noble Eightfold Path (right view, thought, speech, action, livelihood, effort, mindfulness, and samadhi). And what does Laozi prescribe? *Be as dust. A profound unity.*

Ironically, when we attain this level of enlightenment, we do not appear aloof to other people. We are centered, uncomplicated, and trustworthy. Thus, we are *the most highly revered.*

VERSE 57. DON'T MEDDLE

Chartres Cathedral, France

57 五十七

yǐ zhēng zhì guó	以正治国
yǐ jī yòng bīng	以奇用兵
yǐ wú shì qǔ tiān xià	以无事取天下
wú hé yǐ zhī qí rán zāi	吾何以知其然哉
yǐ cǐ	以此
tiān xià duō jì huì ér mín mí pín	天下多忌讳而民弥贫
mín duō lì qì guó jiā zī hūn	民多利器国家滋昏
rén duō jì qiǎo jī wù xuān qǐ	人多伎巧奇物滋起
fǎ lìng zī zhāng dào zéi duō yǒu	法令滋彰盗贼多有
gù shèng rén yún	故圣人云
wǒ wú wéi ér mín zì huā	我无为而民自化
wǒ hǎo jìng ér mín zì zhēng	我好静而民自正
wǒ wú shì ér mín zì fù	我无事而民自富
wǒ wú yù ér mín zì pǔ	我无欲而民自朴

Be straightforward in ruling a nation
Be unpredictable in war
Use not-doing in dealing with the natural world

I know this because
the more prohibitions and laws are enacted
    the poorer the people become
The more heavily the government arms itself
    the more the people will riot
As people become more ingenious and crafty
    the stranger they behave
The more calls are made for law and order
    the more robbers and bandits abound

So the wise say
Practice not-doing
    and the people will thrive independently
Invite quietness
    and the people will calm by themselves
Don't meddle
    and the people will prosper freely
Be restrained
    and the people will enjoy a simple and happy life

Verses 57–60 and 72–75 all address government, and I think they make sense as either eight short verses or two long ones. It is important to pause and remember Laozi's environment and historical time frame here because things can get a little strange on the subjects of politics, leadership, and government. His prescience in some areas is remarkable. In psychology, for example, Laozi can sound contemporary. In politics, however, a few things have happened since his time—democracy, for example—that can make his politics look a little outdated.

These verses would look quite different, I am sure, had Laozi witnessed democracies in action, although as Winston Churchill said at a speech on Armistice Day in 1947, democracies are far from perfect: "Democracy is the worst possible form of government—apart from all those others that have been tried from time to time." And Plato, an approximate contemporary of Laozi, who had witnessed democracy in ancient Greece, said, "Democracy is a charming form of government, full of variety and disorder, and dispensing a sort of equality to equals and unequals alike." Or as H. L. Mencken said in 1956, not realizing he was prophesying Donald Trump, "As democracy is perfected, the office of president represents, more and more closely, the inner soul of the people. On some great and glorious day, the plain folks of the land will reach their heart's desire at last, and the White House will be adorned by a downright moron."

And from the strange vantage point of 2025, in a world of Trump's America, Victor Orbán's Hungary, and Recep Tayyip Erdoğan's Turkey, perhaps we shouldn't be so smug about the greatness of democracy. Yes, it has been very effective in many countries, but it no longer looks inevitable. For a while there, it looked as though democracy would go from country to country, strength to strength, and would deliver more and more freedoms. Now, it looks a little bogged down. A close examination is required to find ways to build stable democracies, but not only that. We also need genuine cooperation among nations to fight global inequities and prevent global environmental catastrophe, and none of the systems we have tried—from time to time—seem quite up to the task. Global cooperation looked unlikely even with expanding democracies. It looks even less likely as they decline.

It is also worthy of note that China has never known democracy. The country was unified, after a fashion, soon after Laozi's time, by Emperor Qin Shihuang, he of the Terracotta Warriors lunacy, and roiled through the dynastic cycle all the way to the mad communist empire of Mao Zedong. China now finds itself in the midst of the capitalist police state empire of mild-smiling Pooh-bear Emperor Xi Jinping. One might argue that China is one of the least Dao countries in the world right now. *I know this because the more prohibitions and laws are enacted the poorer the people become* and *the more the people will riot.* And *the stranger they behave . . . the more robbers and bandits abound.*

VERSE 58. UNOBTRUSIVE GOVERNMENT

Plum blossoms

58　　五十八

qí zhèng mēn mēn qí mín chún chún　　其政閔閔其民淳淳

qí zhèng chá chá qí mín quē quē　　其政察察其民缺缺

huò shàng fú zhī suǒ yǐ　　祸尚福之所倚

fú shàng huò zhī suǒ fú　　福尚祸之所伏

shú zhī qí jí qí wú zhēng　　孰知其极其无正

zhēng fù wéi jī shàn fù wéi yāo　　复为奇善复为妖

rén zhī mí qí rì gù jiǔ　　人之迷其日固久

shì yǐ shèng rén fāng ér bù gē　　是以圣人方而不割

lián ér bù guì　　廉而不刿

zhí ér bù sì　　直而不肆

guāng ér bù yào　　光而不耀

When government is restrained   unobtrusive
the people will be simple   genuine
When government is severe   prying
the people will be needy   cunning

Happiness teeters above misery
Misery lurks beneath happiness
Who knows which is in the future?

Without guidance
the upright revert to evil
and confusion and anarchy reign

So the wise are
sharp without being cutting
pointed without piercing
assertive without bullying
and brilliant without dazzling

The overarching theme of verses 57–60 is *wuwei* in leadership. In verse 57, Laozi argued that leaders should practice *wuwei* by inviting *quietness*, avoiding micromanagement, and being *restrained*. When this hands-off leadership approach is employed, *the people with thrive*. They will *calm themselves, prosper freely*, and *enjoy a simple and happy life*.

Verse 58 continues this message. The goal is a peaceful society in which people are *simple* and *genuine*, and Laozi argues that this is made possible when the government is *restrained* and *unobtrusive*. The best way to incite trouble among the people, to make them *needy* and *cunning*, is for the government to use a heavy hand, to be *severe* and *prying*.

But it is not enough for a government to do nothing. *Wuwei* does not propose careless inaction or laziness. There is a need to stay connected and to guide people toward the right actions. We mustn't meddle, but neither should we abandon things that need attention. *Without guidance, confusion and anarchy reign.*

I hear a somewhat Libertarian voice from Laozi in a call for small government and limited intervention, but he does believe in government. Its role is not to promote an ideology but instead to govern: to do stuff, to organize things, fix things, provide services, and coordinate public works. The wise government does practical things properly, organizes well, and does so without overt display or unnecessary demands.

The wise, meanwhile, are effective, and intelligent—*sharp*—but not sarcastic, demeaning, or arrogant about their intellectual prowess; they are not *cutting*. They demonstrate things that must be done, tell the truth, and enact laws, but they don't cause pain or humiliation: *they are pointed without piercing*. The wise insist that the right path be followed. If a public works must be organized or a law must be followed or if a societal rule has been broken or defied, the wise are *assertive* without being aggressive or *bullying*. And the wise, to find this balance where exactly the right amount of attention, guidance, and assertion, must be *brilliant*, but they should not *be dazzling*. They should be unobtrusive.

The watchword here is "balance," because, after all, the line between good and evil is not always clear. *Happiness teeters above misery* and *misery lurks beneath happiness, and who knows which is in the future?*

VERSE 59. LEAD WITH MODERATION

Hạ Long Bay, Vietnam

59　五十九

zhì rén shì tiān mò ruò sè	治 人 事 天 莫 苦 啬
fū wéi sè shì wéi zǎo fú	夫 唯 啬 是 谓 早 服
zǎo fú wéi zhī chóng jī dé	早 服 谓 之 重 积 德
chóng jī dé zé wú bù kè	重 积 德 则 无 不 克
wú bù kè zé mò zhī qí jí	无 不 克 则 莫 知 其 极
mò zhī qí jí kě yǐ yǒu guó	莫 知 其 极 可 以 有 国
yǒu guó zhī mǔ kě yǐ cháng jiǔ	有 国 之 母 可 以 长 久
shì wéi shēn gēn gù dǐ	是 谓 深 根 固 柢
cháng shēng jiǔ shì zhī dào	长 生 久 视 之 道

In governing show moderation
    like a farmer storing grain
    like living off the land
Live sparingly and flexibly
This is what it is to accumulate virtue

With abundant virtue
    everything can be overcome
    anything can be achieved
and you are fit to rule
Rule like the mother
and you will rule long

Have deep roots and a solid base
This is the Path of longevity and clarity

Some leaders are genuinely good people. They do a good job, and at the end of their term they step away. They are precious—and rare. Some leaders begin evil, stay evil, and die ugly. They want power for their own benefit; they cling to it, and it often ends them. These parasites don't actually interest me all that much—and there are far too many of them. The leaders who fascinate me are the ones who begin as heroes but lose their way and end up as despots. What happens to them? Perhaps they only seemed heroic and were always intent on despotism, but I think there have been some good examples of the hero breaking bad.

Some of the communist leaders of the twentieth century fall into this category. Fidel Castro, for example, seems to have been genuine at first. He led a scrappy, underdog revolution against a horrible regime. He seems to have tried hard to set up a government that would lift Cubans out of poverty and free them from the clutches of American imperialism, and his government was successful in many areas: health care and education, for example. But as his government struggled, he defended his ideology with increasing brutality and became more and more the despot he had once deposed. China's Mao Zedong might represent a similar transition: a hero of the revolution with a desire to create a more equitable society, a narcissistic response to failure and a paranoid outlook against dissenters, and a brief moment as "Emperor of Communist China" ending in a legacy as a monster despite Xi Jinping's crusade to rewrite history. (Emperor Xi doesn't interest me all that much.)

Laozi urges moderation in leadership, *like a farmer storing grain*, and urges leaders to accumulate virtue by living *sparingly and flexibly*. Many leaders have tried to be this way at first but have proven unable to maintain their humility for the long run. Before too long they have found themselves wearing their simple "I am one of you" workingman's garb in a palace. Juan Perón's *descamisado* routine comes to mind.

The utmost moderation comes from following the Dao, which can guide anyone but might be particularly valuable for leaders. Leadership has a habit of changing people in unpleasant ways: power corrupts, and absolute power corrupts absolutely. Perhaps leaders go astray because they cannot trust people as easily, fearing treachery. Perhaps that's because they have been treacherous themselves. Whatever the reasons, Laozi has particular concern for the virtues of leaders. They must have *deep roots and a solid base*. In Laozi's view, *this is the path to longevity and clarity*.

VERSE 60. LET SLEEPING DOGS LIE

Alleyway, Prague Old Town, Czechia

60　六十

zhì dà guó ruò pēng xiǎo xiān　治大国若烹小鲜

yǐ dào lì tiān xià　以道莅天下

qí guǐ bù shén　其鬼不神

fēi qí guǐ bù shén　非其鬼不神

qí shén bù shāng rén　其神不伤人

fēi qí shén bù shāng rén　非其神不伤人

shèng rén yì bù shāng rén　圣人亦不伤人

fū liǎng bù xiāng shāng　夫两不相伤

gù dé jiāo guī yān　故德交归焉

Governing a big country
is like cooking a small fish

Govern in accordance with the Dao
and the evil spirits will be left asleep
They are always there
but the wise can step quietly around them

If evil has no reason to flourish
the wise have no reason to intervene

Governing a big country is like cooking a small fish. Isn't that a great line? Don't fiddle with it, don't fuss with it, and don't overcook it.

The second stanza introduces the idea of evil spirits. Who are these evil spirits? It is not entirely clear who or what they are, but we are advised that they should be left asleep, and Chinese folklore has some of the most fabulously garish evil spirits. You don't want to mess with them. There are dragons, of course, plenty of them, and there is the Aoyin, a West China cannibal; Baigujing, literally White Bones Lady, a skeleton who'll eat you to become immortal; a menacing black fog; a drowned grandma; dog demons; and Hulijing, a creepy oversexed fox.

The evil spirits . . . are always there but the wise can step quietly around them reminds me of a wonderful scene from the Leon Gast documentary about Muhammad Ali, *When We Were Kings,*[21] in which Malik Bowens compares Ali to a sleeping elephant after the "Rumble in the Jungle," his famous fight against George Foreman in Kinshasa. Ali went to the ropes, allowed Foreman to punch himself out, and then rose from the ropes in the seventh round to knock Foreman down. Bowens said, "You can do whatever you want around a sleeping elephant, but once he awakens, he will trample everything in his path."

That a government might awaken evil spirits was made obvious to Americans during the first Donald Trump presidency. We know there are terrible racists and white supremacists in America; it is part of our history. The country was founded on the extermination and dispossession of Indigenous Americans and the enslavement of people of African heritage: two of the world's worst genocides. Trump didn't create racism in America, but he did reawaken it. Government has the potential to bring out the best in people. It can bring us together, but it can also tear us apart and unearth our ghosts. Our history is rife with stories of evil deeds in evil times, which, in peaceful times, are difficult to comprehend.

And these evil spirits are not always others. We must also recognize that Abraham Lincoln's "better angels of our nature" reside alongside our own demons. We must choose whether to revive the angels and let the demons sleep or bring the demons to life. Or, as Alexandr Solzhenitsyn said, "If only it were all so simple! If only there were evil people somewhere insidiously committing evil deeds, and it were necessary only to separate them from the rest of us and destroy them. But the line dividing good and evil cuts through the heart of each human being. And who is willing to destroy a piece of his own heart?"[22]

VERSE 61. SPRING AND AUTUMN: WARRING STATES

Swamp

61　六十一

dà guó zhě xià liú tiān xià zhī jiāo	大国者下流天下之交
tiān xià zhī pìn pìn cháng yǐ jìng shèng mǔ	天下之牝常以静胜牡
yǐ jìng wéi xià	以静为下
gù dà guó yǐ xià xiǎo guó	故大国以下小国
zé qǔ xiǎo guó	则取小国
xiǎo guó yǐ xià dà guó	小国以下大国
zé qǔ dà guó	则取大国
gù huò xià yǐ qǔ	故或下以取
huò xià ér qǔ	或下而取
dà guó bù guò yù jiān chù rén	大国不过欲兼畜人
xiǎo guó bù guò yù rù shì rén	小国不过欲入事人
fū liǎng zhě gè dé suǒ yù	夫两者各得所欲
dà zhě yí wéi xià	大者宜为下

A great nation is the delta
at the end of the valley
the lowest point
where the river merges with the sea

Consider the female
Quieter than the male
she takes the lower position
and yet surmounts him

If a small country yields to a great one
it will be annexed
If a small country conquers a large one
it will eventually be absorbed

Some who yield conquer
Some who yield are conquered
A great nation needs more people
A small nation needs to serve

Both can have their way
It is fitting to yield and merge

The *Daodejing* was laid down during the Zhou dynasty, which is divided into two periods: the rather pleasant-sounding Spring and Autumn period and the decidedly less appealing Warring States period. In Laozi's time, unity and stability must have seemed like pipe dreams as the warlords of China fought ruthlessly and frequently for territory. China was a hot mess of seven warring states in his time, the Chu, Han, Qi, Qin, Wei, Yan, and Zhao. It would soon be unified under the short-lived Qin dynasty following the brutal conquests of Emperor Qin Shihuang, he of Terracotta Warriors fame. This guy built a massive mausoleum complex replete with magnificent heaven-traveling chariot and a ten thousand–strong life-size terracotta army to guide him into the afterlife. He then murdered or blinded all the folks who had worked on the tomb complex in hopes that it would remain secret and safe as he voyaged through the heavens. Definitely a contender for the title of worst human ever.

Laozi describes conflicts among nations and territories in ways that will not be to everybody's liking: one man's terrorist is another man's freedom fighter, they say. The *great nation is the delta* with which the rivers of smaller nations merge. A small nation will be merged into a large one if it is defeated, which is easy to picture, but it will become merged even if it is victorious because its culture will eventually be subsumed into that of the larger one. Conflict, in Laozi's view, is unnecessary, and it is natural for nations to merge. He seems to have believed that the joining of nations to form larger unions was an entirely natural and desirable thing. He would probably have taken a dim view of those who fought for independence or for the sovereignty of culturally unique nations.

This is my least favorite verse in the *Daodejing*. I think it is completely valid for small nations to demand their sovereignty and defend their cultural identity. I also dislike the use of the submissive but controlling woman as an object of metaphor in this verse. The image *she takes the lower position and yet surmounts him* clearly plays on the demeaning notion of trading sex for influence.

Ukrainians will not like this verse as they attempt to oust "Tsar" Vladimir Putin from their country, nor will Taiwanese, Tibetans, and Hongkongese living in the thrall of Emperor Xi, and nor will people aligned with separatist movements in Catalonia, Western Sahara, Quebec, Nagorno-Karabakh, and Scotland, but Laozi puts peace and stability above independence. The protection of unique expressions of diversity and culture is not his shtick. Laozi says, *It is fitting to yield and merge.* He is less concerned by who wins or loses than with the hope that antagonists can come together, because he sees it as inevitable that, one way or another, they should.

VERSE 62. THE
GREATEST GIFT

Runoff from Prismatic Spring, Yellowstone National Park, Wyoming

62　六十二

dào zhě wàn wù zhī ào	道者万物之奥
shàn rén zhī bǎo bù shàn rén zhī suǒ bǎo	善人之宝不善人之所保
měi yán kě yǐ shì zūn	美言可以市尊
měi xíng kě yǐ jiā rén	美行可以加人
rén zhī bù shàn hé qì zhī yǒu	人之不善何弃之有
gù lì tiān zǐ zhì sān gōng	故立天子置三公
suī yǒu gǒng bì yǐ xiān sì mǎ	虽有拱璧以先驷马
bù rú zuò jìn cǐ dào	不如坐进此道
gǔ zhī suǒ yǐ guì cǐ dào zhě hé	古之所以贵此道者何
bù yuē qiú yǐ dé	不曰求以得
yǒu zuì yǐ miǎn xié	有罪以免邪
gù wéi tiān xià guì	故为天下贵

Dao is the refuge of all things
Treasure for the noble
Protection for the wicked

Beautiful words earn admiration
Good deeds win respect
but those lacking beautiful words
    and good deeds
why would the Dao abandon them?

So at the coronation of the emperor
or the investiture of the three ministers
where a gift of fine jade might be made
    or a team of four horses

kneel instead
humbly
and offer to teach
the Way   the Dao

The ancients valued the Dao highly
They said
Seek   and you will find
Offend   and you will be forgiven

Thus is the Dao a gift of the world

The saying "seek, and you will find; offend, and you will be forgiven" reminds me of the Sermon on the Mount: "Ask, and it shall be given; seek, and you shall find; knock, and the door shall be opened to you" (Matthew 7:7–8). As an aside, it is remarkable how little Jesus figures in the Bible. There are only a handful of significant moments in his short adult life between the first ministries in small Galilean villages and his crucifixion as an insurgent against the Roman Empire in Jerusalem. The Sermon on the Mount is one of these few moments—and probably the best—when his philosophy truly shines. It should not be surprising, then, that so much of this ancient text parallels others. All ancient texts have promised to be the greatest gift in the way Laozi makes the claim here for the *Daodejing*.

I am amused by the image of some poor guy showing up at the palace and saying "Well, your Highness, I was going to get you a team of four horses for your birthday, but instead I'm going to give you a little sage advice" (Off with his head!), or, at home, "Well, Honey, I was going to get you some beautiful jade jewelry for your birthday, but, well, I've noticed you've been a bit tense lately, so here's a little sage advice" (Off with his testicles!).

It truly is a gift to be able to understand oneself, sense one's place in the cosmos, and be able to manage one's mind. But is this a gift that can be given? I don't think so. You can lead a horse to water, they say, but you cannot make it drink. And I sense that gifts of this kind often reflect the needs of the giver more than those of the recipient. We tend to think that what brings enlightenment to us will bring enlightenment to others, but that might be rather arrogant. I'm thinking of those poor Mormon kids sent out to spend a good part of their young lives pushing a dodgy ideology around dodgy neighborhoods in a dodgy black pants, white shirt, gold name badge uniform and the Jehovah's Witness folks schlepping *The Watchtower* from door to door to door (and eyeroll to eyeroll to eyeroll). Bless their little hearts.

But there do seem to be some universal truths, and perhaps there are multiple paths to them—or perhaps there are multiple ways to find the path. That so many people claim they have insights that can teach others might indicate that humans are universally arrogant, but it might also mean that there is indeed a universal opportunity to find personal enlightenment. The doors to it may be many. Your door isn't all that special. Many people will find a door that works for them, and if they do it is unlikely to look like yours. Nonetheless, helping people find their own door might indeed be quite the gift.

VERSE 63. *WUWEI, WUSHI*

Cloudy canyon, Yellow Mountains

63 六十三

wéi wú wéi	为 无 为
shì wú shì	事 无 事
wèi wú wèi	味 无 味
dà xiǎo duō shǎo	大 小 多 少
bào yuàn yǐ dé	报 怨 以 德
tú nán yú qí yì	图 难 于 其 易
wéi dà yú qí xì	为 大 于 其 细
tiān xià nán shì bì zuò yú yì	天 下 难 事 必 作 于 易
tiān xià dà shì bì zuò yú xì	天 下 大 事 必 作 于 细
shì yǐ shèng rén zhōng bù wéi dà	是 以 圣 人 终 不 为 大
gù néng chéng qí dà	故 能 成 其 大
fū qīng nuò bì guǎ xìn	夫 轻 诺 必 寡 信
duō yì bì duō nán	多 易 必 多 难
shì yǐ shèng rén yóu nán zhī	是 以 圣 人 犹 难 之
gù zhōng wú nán yǐ	故 终 无 难 矣

Do without doing
Act without acting
Find flavor in the bland

To big or small
to many or few
respond to vice with virtue

Tackle the difficult in its simplest form
Tackle big problems while they are small
Difficult problems arise from simple ones
Big problems arise from small ones
So the wise
    do not struggle with big problems
    and yet they solve them

Frivolous promises negate trust
Halfhearted work creates complications
So the wise
    by treating the easy as hard
    find everything easy

Do without doing	wéi wú wéi	为 无 为
Act without acting	shì wú shì	事 无 事
[Taste not taste]	wèi wú wèi	味 无 味

We return to a verse centered on *wuwei* and, I think, one of the best expositions of *wuwei* in the *Daodejing*. The verse begins with a doubling of *wuwei* by emphasizing it with *wushi*. The third line is a little difficult to translate and interpret, and I suspect it was included for the satisfaction of the rhyme rather than the meaning. Phonetically, the line reads *wei wu wei*, just like the first line, but means "taste not taste" or "flavor not flavor." I translate it as *find flavor in the bland*, but I think it is included just as a little play on word sounds.

The middle of the verse gives practical advice in achieving *wuwei*. These are simple tactics for making your life easier by being more effective while struggling less. They are life hacks for the situations in which "slow down, do less" will make you more productive. Laozi advises that we tackle problems early and in their simplest form. It is simple advice and obvious, but we often fail to follow it. Change your oil every five thousand miles. Go to the dentist every six months. That lump? Get it checked out immediately because *big problems arise from small ones*. The wise solve problems before they become big ones and so they don't have to struggle. The wise are also careful about what they promise and conscientious about doing quality work. Thus, *by treating everything as hard*, they *find everything easy*.

My favorite line in this verse and one of the best in the *Daodejing* is *respond to vice with virtue*. It is simply lovely and is the ultimate expression of forgiveness and a powerful guide to nonviolent resistance. It has been translated in slightly different ways by different authors, all of them equally wonderful: *Requites injuries with good deeds* (Waley), *Meet injury with the power of goodness* (Le Guin), *Requite hatred with goodness* (Carus), *Reward bitterness with care* (Feng and English). And this rule to *respond to vice with virtue* applies to everyone: *to big or small* and *to many or few*. Don't puff yourself up for the boss, and don't boss your employee around. Treat the CEO and the janitor the same.

As we have seen with many other verses, it is not at all clear that the conventional division of the book into eighty-one verses is ideal. This verse flows directly into the next one.

VERSE 64. ACT, DON'T REACT

Pat, Sam, and Dan, Celery Bog sunset, West Lafayette, Indiana

64 六十四

qí ān yì chí qí wèi zhào yì móu	其安易持其未兆易谋
qí cuì yì pàn qí wēi yì sàn	其脆易泮其微易散
wéi zhī yú wèi yǒu zhì zhī yú wèi luàn	为之于未有治之于未乱
hé bào zhī mù shēng yú háo mò	合抱之木生于毫末
jiǔ céng zhī tái qǐ yú léi tǔ	九层之台起于累土
qiān lǐ zhī xíng shǐ yú zú xià	千里之行始于足下
wéi zhě bài zhī zhí zhě shī zhī	为者败之执者失之
shì yǐ shèng rén wú wéi gù wú bài	是以圣人无为故无败
wú zhí gù wú shī	无执故无失
mín zhī cóng shì cháng yú jǐ chéng ér bài zhī	民之从事常于几成而败之
shèn zhōng rú shǐ zé wú bài shì	慎终如始则无败事
shì yǐ shèng rén yù bù yù	是以圣人欲不欲
bù guì nán dé zhī huò	不贵难得之货
xué bù xué fù zhòng rén zhī suǒ guò	学不学复众人之所过
yǐ fǔ wàn wù zhī zì rán ér bù gǎn wéi	以辅万物之自然而不敢为

That which is settled is easily maintained
That which still develops is easily managed
The brittle is easily broken
The small is easily scattered

Act before problems develop
Govern well before disorder emerges

The massive tree first grows as a sapling
The tall tower is built from a pile of bricks
The journey of a thousand miles begins
    with a single step

Those who act cause harm
Those who snatch fumble
So the wise
    leave things alone to avoid causing harm
    and don't snatch at things to avoid dropping them
(The unwise often fail near the end
Take care at endings as much as in beginnings)

The wise do not desire desires
    nor treasure treasures
They learn to unlearn
    so they can restore to people
    what they have overlooked

Thus they return everything to its true nature
    and dare not act

We pick up where we left off in the previous verse with a reiteration of the importance of timely action. *That which is settled is easily maintained. That which still develops is easily managed.* It is a reminder that keeping on top of things is much more relaxing and effective than wrestling with problems that were allowed to get out of control. Laozi might be giving advice to emperors, presidents, and prime ministers, but he might also be talking to gardeners or farmers. It is the perfect advice in controlling weeds, for example. *Act before problems develop. Govern well before disorder emerges.* The best weed control slices tiny seedlings with a sharp, light hoe, rather than trying to wrestle deeply rooted thickets from the ground.

All big things start small, as one of Laozi's best-known memes tells us: *The journey of a thousand miles begins with a single step.* So, as well as tackling emerging problems early, we should also be aware that many things take time to develop and mature. All cultures have sayings such as "patience is a virtue," and this is reiterated in the next stanza: *Those who act do harm. Those who snatch fumble.* And just as long processes must be handled patiently and be allowed to develop in their own time, so too must we remain patient and follow them to their conclusions: *The unwise often fail near the end. Take care at endings as much as in beginnings.* This is all lovely practical advice in the art of *wuwei* living. And we are also reminded of the source of all our mental instability and suffering: cravings and desires. *The wise do not desire desires nor treasure treasures.*

The verse ends with the rather enigmatic statement that *the wise . . . dare not act.* This seems unnecessarily tentative after everything that has come before. We have learned to tackle things early, to watch them as they develop, to intervene only with caution, and to follow things through to the end to make sure they are completed perfectly, and then, after all this, we are advised not to act at all.

The first rule of ecology should be "You can never do one thing." Importing cane toads to eat bugs in the sugarcane fields seemed smart until the toads ignored the cane bugs and started scoffing down everything else. Planting kudzu to manage roadside soil erosion seemed like a good idea until kudzu became "the plant that ate the South." Ditto myriad invasives: silver carp, brown tree snakes, zebra mussels, prickly pear, and Paterson's curse. A hydroelectric dam might seem like an indisputable good that produces clean energy, controls life-threatening floods, and provides irrigation water, but it may prevent fish migrations, change the ecology of the river, and affect the long-term fertility of downstream valleys. Our knowledge, or presumed knowledge, of systems can result in a hubristic sense of having control over nature. It is much more sensible is to *return everything to its true nature* by not acting, because if we don't act there is less risk that we will later need to react.

VERSE 65. BE WARY
OF CLEVERNESS

Jewish Cemetery, Prague, Czechia

65 六十五

gǔ zhī shàn wéi dào zhě fēi yǐ míng mín
古之善为道者非以明民

jiāng yǐ yú zhī
将以愚之

mín zhī nán zhì yǐ qí zhì duō
民之难治以其智多

gù yǐ zhì zhì guó guó zhī zéi
故以智治国国之贼

bù yǐ zhì zhì guó guó zhī fú
不以智治国国之福

zhī cǐ liǎng zhě yì jī shì
知此两者亦稽式

cháng zhī jī shì
常知稽式

shì wèi xuán dé
是谓玄德

xuán dé shēn yǐ yuǎn yǐ yú wù fǎn yǐ
玄德深矣远矣与物反矣

rán hòu nǎi zhì dà shùn
然后乃至大顺

The ancients were devoted followers of the Path
They were cautious when teaching the people
Knowledge can encourage craftiness
and crafty people can be difficult to govern

Likewise it is deceitful to use trickery to govern
Governing without trickery is a great blessing

To see this is to see a deeper pattern
a deeper pattern that leads to profound virtue
profound virtue that reaches far back
into the place to which everything returns
where everything is guided
toward order and unity

Have you ever had an argument with someone and noticed that they weren't really listening to you? Of course you have: it's common. Sometimes you'll get the distinct impression that the other person is simply waiting for a break in the conversation so they can slot in their next argument. They already know what they're going to say next, and it may have nothing to do with what you're saying now. Of course, it's not just *they*, it's also me—and it's also you. It only takes cleverness to win an argument. It takes wisdom to learn from one.

To learn from an argument—or speech or conversation—you actually have to listen, and so the only time you can win from arguing is when you are listening well enough to be able to concede points to the other person. You cannot win an argument by out-stubborning the other person. You only win when you learn. And if you listen attentively and debate honestly, there is also a chance that you might teach something, which was presumably your goal all along.

Trickery in arguments benefits nobody, and knowledge without wisdom can encourage people to be crafty—and a crafty populace is difficult to govern. The core of the solution, Laozi argues, is to govern without trickery, because *it is deceitful to use trickery to govern. Governing without trickery is a great blessing.* We call it transparency, although promises of it are a dime a dozen while valid examples of it are rare. Our bosses and politicians sometimes deliver and sometimes don't, and when we start to think they are being evasive or dishonest, we become treacherous. Well, I do. I don't need a raise nearly as much as I need to trust that raises are divvied out fairly. I'm usually a cooperative member of society, but put some dumb, sticklerish rule in front of me, and I get decidedly crafty. I can't sit here? This seat is only for fancy people? Oh, yeah? Watch me!

This seems like a fairly simple thing to understand, but Laozi makes a big deal of it. *To see this*, he says, *is to see a deeper pattern that leads to profound virtue.* Profound virtue? It seems like a relatively minor piece of useful advice. But what is it that makes it profound? I think Laozi is reminding us that while this is a simple idea to understand, it is not a simple one to execute. Listening carefully is remarkably difficult. It requires us to exercise nonjudgment, and that can be hard to rouse. But this state of nonjudgment and careful listening leads to much more profound things. According to Laozi, this profound virtue *reaches far back into the place to which everything returns... toward order and unity.* Listening to other people, then, is just the first step. Once you have learned to listen to human beings, you can begin to listen to other beings and the world.

VERSE 66. BLESSED ARE THE MEEK

Windswept woman

66　六十六

hǎi zhī suǒ yǐ néng wéi bǎi gǔ wáng zhě　海之所以能为百谷王者

yǐ qí shàn xià zhī　以其善下之

gù néng wéi bǎi gǔ wáng　故能为百谷王

shì yǐ shèng rén　是以圣人

yù shàng mín bì yǐ yán xià zhī　欲上民必以言下之

yù xiān mín bì yǐ shēn hòu zhī　欲先民必身后之

shì yǐ shèng rén　是以圣人

chǔ shàng ér mín bù chóng　处上而民不重

chǔ qián ér mín bù hài　处前而民不害

shì yǐ tiān xià lè tuī ér bù yàn　是以天下乐推而不厌

yǐ qí bù zhēng　以其不争

gù tiān xià mò néng yú zhī zhēng　故天下莫能与之争

The seas and great rivers are the kings
of the hundred valleys and ravines
They rule by lying below
Water flows down to them
giving the valley shape

So the wise   to stand above
must speak from below
to lead   must follow

So the wise can be placed over people
without being a burden
can be ahead of people
without causing an obstruction
can be praised
without becoming tiresome

The wise do not resist
and thus are not resisted

"Blessed are the meek," said Jesus of Nazareth, "for they shall inherit the Earth" (Matthew 5:5). Or as Michelle Obama said, "When they go low, we go high."

This verse instructs leaders on the importance of humility. *The wise, to stand above, must speak from below; to lead, must follow.* Great leaders must have many characteristics. They must, first of all, be competent. A good leader is not just the one in front, plowing forward, but rather the one who knows the way. Here, Laozi discusses the value of a yin style of leadership and returns to one of his favorite images: water.

Water shapes the valley not because of where it comes from but because of where it is going. Rain falls everywhere but then flows downward through rills, gullies, ravines, and valleys as it traces its inexorable path to the sea. Ultimately, it is what is below the water, and therefore in its future, that guides it, not what is above. And it is the water itself, drawn from below, that shapes the valley. Water erodes faster where the pull of gravity is stronger and cuts deeper into the landscape where its current is fiercer. So, the sea draws the water from the river, the river pulls the water from the streams, and the streams drag the water across the landscape.

The yin leader, knowing the way, directing from below, can be placed *over the people without being a burden, ahead of people without causing an obstruction*, and can be *praised without becoming tiresome*. The yin leader knows how to find the safest and most peaceful path along which to guide her people. There are dangerous paths that should be avoided and challenges that should not be demanded of others. Unlike the yang leader, who chases the path of glory, the yin leader follows the path that is the best for those she leads. *The wise do not resist and thus are not resisted.* The other tricky thing about paths is that sometimes they must be followed and shaped at the same time. The movement of water over the landscape seeks the lowest place (v. 8) which shapes the path that the rest of the stream will follow. This trailblazing is a tricky business, and one's core values become as essential guide.

Why do we keep choosing yang leaders: these reactive, aggressive, pontificating men? It should be obvious by now that thoughtful, deliberative, collaborative women are better leaders. Not always, of course. There will always be the unfortunate Margaret Thatchers, but compare the COVID-19 responses of Donald Trump and Boris Johnson with those of Jacinda Ardern and Sanna Marin. "Oh, Steve," you say, "Stop with your trendy New Age feminist nonsense!" New Age? Trendy? Laozi understood the power of yin leadership in Zhou dynasty China.

VERSE 67. . . . AND THE GREATEST OF THESE IS COMPASSION

Ci bei characters: Compassion

67 六十七

tiān xià jiē wèi wǒ dào dà sì bù xiào 天下皆谓我道大似不肖

fū wéi dà gù sì bù xiào 夫唯大故似不肖

ruò xiào jiǔ yǐ qí xì yě fū 若肖久矣其细也夫

wǒ yǒu sān bǎo chí ér bǎo zhī 我有三宝持而保之

yī yuē cí 一曰慈

èr yuē jiǎn 二曰俭

sān yuē bù gǎn wéi tiān xià xiān 三曰不敢为天下先

cí gù néng yǒng 慈故能勇

jiǎn gù néng guǎng 俭故能广

bù gǎn wéi tiān xià xiān gù néng chéng qì cháng 不敢为天下先故能成器长

jīn shè cí qiě yǒng 今舍慈且勇

shè jiǎn qiě guǎng 舍俭且广

shè hòu qiě xiān 舍后且先

sǐ yǐ 死矣

fū cí yǐ zhàn zé shèng yǐ shǒu zé gù 夫慈以战则胜以守则固

tiān jiāng jiù zhī yǐ cí wèi zhī 天将救之以慈卫之

Everyone says my Dao is great
but it is simply mine   unique
and therefore   for this   great

I have three treasures
that I hold and protect

The first is compassion
The second is moderation
The third is humility

The compassionate can be courageous
The frugal can be generous
The humble can be great leaders

but to be courageous without compassion
to trade moderation for extravagance
to forsake humility in order to win
This is death

Compassion in battle brings victory
Compassion in defense builds strength
Heaven protects with compassion

And now these three remain: faith, hope, and love; and the greatest of these is love.

1 CORINTHIANS (13:13)

Listen with the ears of tolerance / See with the eyes of compassion / Speak using the language of love.

RUMI

Compassion is eulogized by all religions and philosophies, and they all understand its power. The Sanskrit word *daya*, from the root *da*, meaning gift, is usually translated as compassion. It is one of the core practices of Hinduism. *Karuna* (compassion) and *metta* (loving-kindness) are two of the cornerstones of Buddhism and two of the key forms, or foci, of meditation. *Karuna* is thought of as understanding the suffering of others—and for the suffering of all who are trapped in samsara, the great wheel of life. *Metta* is thought of as extending goodwill, care, and consideration to all beings. In Islam, the words *arahman* and *araheem*, from the root *rahman*, both mean "compassion." The sura Al-Rahman, Chapter 55 of the Quran, sometimes called the Bride of the Quran for its poetic beauty, is interpreted as highlighting the mercy and compassion of Allah. The Stoics developed *oikeiosis*, emphasizing the connectedness of all life. In ancient Greece, compassion was Eleos or Elea, a Goddess, the personification of compassion.

Modern experimental psychology and neuroscience have demonstrated the power of compassion to shape not only the activity of the brain but also its structure. Compassion has the power to improve the health of the minds and bodies of others and of ourselves. Being compassionate with ourselves can render our lives much more pleasant, and its effects can be seen in health metrics such as better sleep and lower blood pressure. Be happy. Be kind. It is not complicated.

Laozi spells out much of his philosophy in the simplest of terms here. There are three treasures: compassion, moderation, and humility. These are three treasures of the De, virtue, and the greatest of them is compassion. It has profound powers. *Compassion in battle brings victory* and *in defense builds strength*. The power of compassion in the human realm should not be surprising, suggests Laozi, because *heaven protects with compassion*. Compassion always wins because it is a surefire way to win battles in your own mind. The way out of anger, for example, is not defeating someone else in an argument. It is always, in the end, about finding forgiveness and compassion for others and also for yourself.

VERSE 68. THE
ART OF PEACE

Stones of the Disappeared in the cobbles outside the former homes
of people taken to Nazi concentration camps

68　六十八

shàn wéi shì zhě bù wǔ	善为士者不武
shàn zhàn zhě bù nù	善战者不怒
shàn shèng dí zhě bù yú	善胜敌者不与
shàn yòng rén zhě wéi zhī xià	善用人者为之下
shì wèi bù zhēng zhī dé	是谓不争之德
shì wèi yòng rén zhī lì	是谓用人之力
shì wèi pèi tiān gǔ zhī jí	是谓配天古之极

A good commander doesn't rush ahead
A good warrior doesn't lose his temper
A good leader overcomes without confrontation

The best rulers put themselves below the people
This is the virtue of noncontention
the source of power of strong leaders
in harmony with heaven's Way

Laozi lived through a time of great conflict when China was fragmented into multiple warring states. It would have been impossible for him not to acknowledge the realities of war and conflict. Here, he gives the very practical military advice—*A good commander doesn't rush ahead* and *doesn't lose his temper*—and yet his philosophy is consistently pacifist. The critical line in this verse is a *good leader overcomes without confrontation*, and Laozi is explicitly talking about a military leader or at least a leader with access to military forces, a *good commander* or a *good warrior*. How can this be achieved?

Martin Luther King Jr., the spiritual leader of the American civil rights movement and Nelson Mandela, the spiritual leader of the South African antiapartheid movement, were students of the nonviolent resistance employed by Mohandas K. (Mahatma) Gandhi to oust the British from India. Its origins are deeply embedded in Eastern philosophy. In the *Daodejing*, nonviolence is a form of *wuwei*. In ancient Indian texts, it is ahimsa. In Gandhi's words, "Ahimsa calls for the strength and courage to suffer without retaliation, to receive blows without returning any," and "ahimsa magnifies one's own defects and minimizes those of the opponent. It regards the mote in one's own eye as a beam and the beam in the opponent's eye as a mote."

Wuwei is not doing nothing: it is doing not-doing. Similarly, nonviolent resistance isn't a refusal to resist but instead is a form of resistance. It is an active and purposeful struggle. Nonviolent resistance does not avoid confrontation but instead invites it. But the most important confrontation it forces is the one the aggressor must have with themselves. Nonviolence will not necessarily be met with reason; indeed, it may be met by extreme violence. Nelson Mandela must have known that something like the Sharpeville massacre of March 21, 1960, was possible, and Martin Luther King Jr. must have always feared something like the bombing of the 16th Street Baptist Church in Birmingham, Alabama, because they both knew about the brutality of the British at Dandi during Gandhi's Salt Satyagraha of March 1930. The primary power of nonviolent resistance is that it forces one's adversary into unilateral action, and when that action gets out of control they must look at themselves in the mirror. Through nonviolence, leaders put *themselves below the people* with *virtue of noncontention*. The source of their power is *in harmony with Heaven's Way*. Strength comes from the confidence of being on the right path.

VERSE 69. THE ART OF WAR

Yellowstone National Park, Wyoming

69 六十九

yòng bīng yǒu yán	用兵有言
wú bù gǎn wéi zhǔ ér wéi kè	吾不敢为主而为客
bù gǎn jìn cùn ér tuì chǐ	不敢进寸而退尺
shì wèi xíng wú xíng	是谓行无行
rǎng wú bì	攘无臂
rēng wú dí	扔无敌
zhí wú bīng	执无兵
huò mò dà yú qīng dí	祸莫大于轻敌
qīng dí jī sàng wú bǎo	轻敌几丧吾宝
gù kàng bīng xiāng jiā āi zhě shèng yǐ	故抗兵相加哀者胜矣

The master of war says
"I dare not strike first
but prefer to defend
I dare not advance an inch
but prefer to retreat a foot"

This is to advance without advancing
reach out without striking
confront without attacking
hold your ground without weapons

No mistake is worse
than underestimating your enemy
Underestimating your enemy
can cost you everything

When well-matched armies clash
the side that yields will win

If you know the enemy and yourself you need not fear
    If you know yourself but not the enemy for every victory you will
suffer a defeat
    If you know neither the enemy nor yourself you will succumb
every time
                        SUNZI (SUN-TZU), *THE ART OF WAR*

Laozi and Sunzi were approximate contemporaries, or rather, considering that no such people may have existed, perhaps we should say that the *Daodejing* and the *Art of War* were approximate contemporaries, and they use similar concepts. Sunzi's approach is more direct, more yang, but often similar to Laozi's yin-based approaches to conflict and contention. Laozi repeatedly advocates yielding, inaction, acting from below, and the superiority of soft power over hard power.

An example from English history is the much-mythologized Battle of Agincourt. The English forces came upon a French army twice their size (or more than five times their size, depending on who's telling it) and much more heavily armed. The modest English army annihilated the French by allowing them to rush their seemingly overwhelming cavalry forces into a mire in range of the well-trained English longbowmen. An example from before Laozi's time that he might have been familiar with is the epic Battle of Muye fought in 1046 BCE. The battle marked the end of the Shang dynasty and the beginning of the Zhou dynasty. Again, a seemingly overwhelming yang-oriented force was mastered by a smarter yin force. In this case, the *Book of Odes* tells us that "the forces of Yin-Shang were collected like a forest." They were, however, composed of many enslaved people who eventually fled to the Zhou side, tipping the battle. These two classic battles and many others—Marathon, Cannae, Hastings— suggest that Laozi's contention that *no mistake is worse than underestimating your enemy* is true. Overconfidence in conflict is a strategic and tactical disaster—ask Goliath of Gath (v. 37).

The last four lines—*Underestimating your enemy can cost you everything. When well-matched armies clash the side that yields will win.*—makes me think of Eastern martial arts. Exponents claim that martial arts such as judo, kung fu (gongfu), and tai chi (taiji) function by using the opposing forces of yin and yang against each other. One idea is to use the aggression and force generated by one's opponent against them. The power of their punch is deflected and returned: they lose their balance, and you keep yours.

This is sage advice not just in wartime battle but also in daily battles. The best way to win an argument is to listen more than you speak and to fully understand the viewpoint of your rival. An aggressive argumentative approach tends to harden a rival's stance. A deliberative and open approach may cause your rival to rethink, which is a win. Or maybe you'll learn something from listening, which is also a win.

VERSE 70. PEARLS
BEFORE SWINE

盗人に
とり残されし
窓の月

自覚

Haiku by Zen hermit Ryokan: The thief left it behind / The moon / At my window

70 七十

wú yán shén yì zhī shén yì xíng	吾言甚易知甚易行
tiān xià mò néng zhī mò néng xíng	天下莫能知莫能行
yán yǒu zōng shì yǒu jūn	言有宗事有君
fū wéi wú zhī shì yǐ wǒ bù zhī	夫唯无知是以我不知
zhī wǒ zhě xī zé wǒ zhě guì	知我者希则我者贵
shì yǐ shèng rén pī hè huái yù	是以圣人被褐怀玉

My words are easily understood
    easily followed
and yet none seem to understand them
    none seem to follow them

My words have an origin
    my deeds have a sovereign
If people don't know them
    how can they know me?
The few who do understand
    are precious to me

The wise are sages
    dressed in sack-cloth
    concealing jade at their hearts

As you are now and I have been for the last few years, an unbroken chain of people—a hundred generations of us—has been pondering this masterpiece known as the *Daodejing*. *My words are easily understood*, says Laozi. Well, maybe. They are simple and direct once understood, I suppose, but reaching an understanding of them is far from easy. And they are *easily followed*. Well, again, maybe.

There are certain things we figure out in life that transform our understanding of the world—those behind-the-curtain moments such as when we see the Wizard of Oz pulling the strings. What, there's no Santa Claus? What about the Easter Bunny? No, no, not the Easter Bunny! Suddenly, we figure something out and see the world with a new clarity.

The Museo Galileo in Florence contains an enormous armillary sphere built by Santucci Pomerance. He completed it in 1593 after five years of work. The armillary sphere represents the "universal machine" and models the motion of the heavenly bodies through the cosmos. It is incredible: detailed, brilliant, immaculately crafted, and totally and utterly wrong. The enormous intricacy and complexity of its construction was required because only such detail could do justice to the intricacy and complexity of the math that had been developed to understand the cosmos. All this genius, however, had been built on the flawed assumption that the stars and planets orbit Earth. Once Copernicus had shown us that Earth and the other planets orbit the sun, no astronomer (no competent non-Catholic astronomer) could ever look at the cosmos the same way again. What Copernicus did was make the unseeable seen and the complex simple.

Evolution did this for me. I read Richard Dawkins's *The Selfish Gene* in my late teens. Biology came alive. Dawkins showed me my place on a continuum of life that stretched all the way back to the first microbes and even to the origins of life itself. Heady stuff for a sixteen-year-old.

So, the *Daodejing* is easy to understand and follow? No, I don't think so, but it presents a way of thinking that can open up new ways of seeing ourselves and our place in the cosmos. Anyway, understanding the *Daodejing* at the cognitive level is the easy part. It is a bit of an obtuse thicket at first but opens up, and its message comes through clearly with study. Following its teachings is another matter—and a matter of degree. To find a perfect yin-yang balance; to consistently cede control; to practice *wuwei*, not-doing; to be like *pu,* the uncarved block; to be like *ziran*, nature, self-so; and to resist cravings and desires? To be compassionate, always, and humble and modest? This is a life's work. The wise who break through not only into these understandings but also follow the Path may not show any outward sign of it—*The wise are sages dressed in sackcloth*—but they live in the world with a new clarity—*concealing jade at their hearts.*

VERSE 71. SELF-AWARENESS

Myvatn Lake, Iceland

71   七十一

zhī bù zhī shàng bù zhī zhī bìng	知 不 知 上 不 知 知 病
fū wéi bìng bìng shì yǐ bù bìng	夫 唯 病 病 是 以 不 病
shèng rén bù bìng yǐ qí bìng bìng	圣 人 不 病 以 其 病 病
fū wéi bìng bìng shì yǐ bù bìng	夫 唯 病 病 是 以 不 病

To know your ignorance is good
To be ignorant of your ignorance is a sickness

To be sick of sickness is healthy

The wise see sickness for what it is
and so they are healthy

A number of verses of the *Daodejing* are open to significant differences in translation and interpretation. This one uses only twelve different characters which it rearranges on each line. The meaning is particularly obtuse.

Laozi seems to be talking about mental frailty, not mental illness per se but rather the type of generalized mental suffering that the Buddha called *dukkha*. The wise are people who have a healthy sense of themselves, and I think this verse advocates for the honest appraisal of one's own humdrum mental machinations. We might call this the development of self-awareness. The wisdom of the Buddha might help us again. His understanding of the mundane, everyday mental suffering of human beings is nicely illustrated by the concept of the second dart. The first dart sticks us and causes pain. The first dart is real and unavoidable, but the pain it causes might be short-lived. This could be the end of our suffering, but we often respond to the first dart by throwing a second dart at ourselves. Perhaps we become outraged: "Who threw that?" Perhaps our feelings are hurt: "Why would they throw a dart at me?" Perhaps we are humiliated: "Why do people think so little of me that they would throw this dart?" The vast majority of human pain comes not from first darts but instead from second darts, and their pain is completely avoidable.

This verse is also a tantalizing exposition of the Dunning-Kruger effect, which shows that experts tend to underestimate their knowledge of a field, whereas novices tend to overestimate theirs. The underestimation by experts comes from their understanding that the field is complex, that there might yet be much still to learn. Their expertise gives them humility: "the more I learn the less I know." *To know your ignorance is good.* Novices, meanwhile, haven't yet studied the field closely, so they tend to think it is easier than it is. As Alexander Pope said, "Fools rush in where angels fear to tread." *To be ignorant of your ignorance is a sickness.*

The problem with all of this is that the self-awareness required to understand the mind and then manage the cognitive and emotional states of the mind is all performed by the very same mind. Why would the mind, if it were to analyze itself, conclude that its sickness was caused by itself—its self? *To know your ignorance is good*, but is shockingly difficult. To delve into the ways of your own mind and openly question its biases, dogmas, opinions, ideologies, gaps, glitches, and, well, sicknesses is to see the mind, your mind, for what it is. This is a bit scary but very healthy. *The wise see sickness for what it is, and so they are healthy.*

VERSE 72. OPPRESSION CAN SEED REVOLUTION

Organoponico Vivero in Alamar, Cuba

72　七十二

mín bù wèi wēi	民 不 畏 威
zé dà wēi zhì	则 大 威 至
wú xiá qí suǒ jū	无 狎 其 所 居
wú yàn qí suǒ shēng	无 厌 其 所 生
fū wéi bù yàn	夫 唯 不 厌
shì yǐ bù yàn	是 以 不 厌
shì yǐ shèng rén	是 以 圣 人
zì zhī bù zì jiàn	自 知 不 自 见
zì ài bù zì guì	自 爱 不 自 贵
gù qù bǐ qǔ cǐ	故 去 彼 取 此

If the people weary of authority
a great force will be unleashed

Don't constrict their lives
Don't limit their livelihoods
Don't show them contempt
and they will not weary of you

The wise love themselves without vanity
know themselves without arrogance

They let go of that
and choose this

The next four verses address tyranny in various ways. They are, you will find, uncomfortably prescient for our modern world.

Saudi Arabia still has a monarchy with bloodline inheritance, as do Brunei, Oman, and Qatar. Dictators still rule thirty-six countries in 2025, including many in Africa and the Middle East. The Arab Spring gave us great hope in 2010–2012 until it was snuffed out and the dictators who survived it quickly doubled down on securing their power. Bashar Al-Assad chose to destroy Syria rather than relinquish power—truly a king to rule over the ashes. And the encroachment of crazies into Europe is disturbing. I think Hungary's Victor Orbán is the one who creeps me out the most. And then there are the "Big Three": China's Emperor Xi Jinping, dictator of a one-party state in the world's most populous country and second-biggest economy; Russia's "tsar" Vladimir Putin, dictator of a new wannabe Russian Empire; and Donald Trump. What a poisonous and narcissistic little bastard he is. We'll find out in coming years just how much harm one monster can do. Many people living in the 2020s who have never known tyranny are beginning to worry.

Tyrants were probably no mystery to Laozi. The time in which he lived was so full of strife and tin-pot dictators that it became known as the Warring States period of the Zhou dynasty. In the end, it yielded to the murderous emperor Qin Shihuang, who is one of history's archetypal mad kings.

This verse opens with a sequence of warnings to dictators. *If the people weary of authority a great force will be unleashed.* This is straightforward enough. Push the people too hard, and you may find yourself with a revolution on your hands—and as much as Laozi speaks against inadequate leaders, he is no fan of revolution. He tells leaders how to avoid the people wearying of them. It is not complicated: *Don't constrict their lives. Don't limit their livelihoods. Don't show them contempt.*

A special place in history is reserved for contemptuous leaders. Things tend to go badly when the masses finally come for them. Nicolae and Elena Ceaușescu ended up riddled with bullets at a military headquarters on December 25, 1989, after the so-called Christmas Revolution. Tsar Nicholas II wound up in a basement in Yekaterinburg where he, his wife, his five children, and a four of the family's imperial entourage were shot at close range and stabbed with bayonets. Marie Antoinette, the wife of Louis XVI of France (probably never) said "Let them eat cake," so they sliced both their heads off with "Madame la Guillotine." English peasants never quite got to King Richard in 1381, but the revolting English peasants got their hands on a few nobles. Simon Sudbury's neck was hacked at with blunt farming implements until his head was separated from his body.

VERSE 73. DARE TO BE PACIFIST

Fishermen near Aurangabad, India

73 七十三

yǒng yú gǎn zé shā 勇于敢则杀

yǒng yú bù gǎn zé huó 勇于不敢则活

cǐ liǎng zhě huò lì huò hài 此两者或利或害

tiān zhī suǒ ě shú zhī qí gù 天之所恶孰知其故

tiān zhī dào bù zhēng ér shàn shèng 天之道不争而善胜

bù yán ér shàn yīng 不言而善应

bù shào ér zì lái 不召而自来

chán rán ér shàn móu 繟然而善谋

tiān wǎng huī huī shū ér bù shī 天网恢恢疏而不失

Rash courage can be fatal
The courage to resist can be liberating

Similar things
Very different outcomes

When heaven provokes failure
who knows the reason?

Heaven's Path
doesn't strive   and yet ably wins
doesn't speak   but answers fully
doesn't call   and yet responds
doesn't rush   but plans calmly

Heaven's net is vast
    wide-meshed
but it misses nothing

I am firmly with Laozi on this one. I get so tired of all the "our brave men and women in uniform" talk. Maybe they're brave and maybe they're not, I don't know, but I find the glorification of the military distasteful. And there's something quite insidious about the way we revere "our courageous soldiers" without doing nearly enough to protect them or care for them. *Rash courage can be fatal.* There's also something quite fake about the whole thing. I don't doubt that it is terrifying to fight in lethal combat, but I also don't doubt that it can take courage to refuse to fight in the first place. It takes a special kind of courage to go against your in-group, especially when their blood lust is up. Standing against the mob by refusing to fight might take more courage than showing up. Heading off to war to join the group in a fight might seem courageous, but Laozi posits it as a form of cowardice from a weakness of mind that causes people to move with the herd. Many people choose to go to war because they lack the courage to take a stand against it. *The courage to resist can be liberating.* It takes courage to go against the crowd. It takes courage to resist, but doing so can be liberating. Laozi is encouraging us to show the bravery required to resist the violence that so often comes when we follow the madding crowd. Rash courage is not courage. Rash courage is a fool's manifestation of craving and desire.

War is awful, we all agree, and yet, secretly and not so secretly, we also love it. War is exciting. It is an adventure. It is great material for a movie. We acclaim those who go to war as courageous, but that's the big lie. The ones with courage are those who refuse to be led by the emotions of the crowd. The ones with courage remain calm in the storm and have the courage to resist.

And then we return to the central theme of the Dao, which is to observe how nature achieves things that are far beyond our powers and does so without fuss. Laozi is urging us—again and again—to observe and emulate nature. None of your angst is needed. Nor does it help in any way. Nor does your anger or urgency. Why are you so anxious to fight? Nature *doesn't strive and yet ably wins.* Why is everything so urgent? Nature *doesn't rush but plans calmly.*

And putting these two themes together, doesn't it seem sometimes as if humans are in some kind of war against nature? All of life is in competition of one kind or another, but the struggles are usually quite specific. Lions with gazelles, caterpillars with cabbages, phages with bacteria. The ever-coevolving struggle between lions and gazelles doesn't usually spill over into caterpillars and cabbages. Humans, on the other hand, seem to feel as though they must have everything under their control: lions, caterpillars, bacteria, and all. Why? And what do we think we could possibly stand to win when we go to war with nature?

VERSE 74. THE GREAT EXECUTIONER

Outside Svalbardseyri, Iceland

74　七十四

mín bù wèi sǐ nài hé yǐ sǐ jù zhī　民不畏死奈何以死惧之

ruò shǐ mín cháng wèi sǐ ér wéi jī zhě　若使民常畏死而为奇者

wú dé zhí ér shā zhī shú gǎn　吾得执而杀之孰敢

cháng yǒu sī shā zhě shā　常有司杀者杀

fū dài sī shā zhě shā　夫代司杀者杀

shì wèi dài dà jiàng zhuó　是谓代大匠斲

fū dài dà jiàng zhuó zhě　夫代大匠斲者

xī yǒu bù shāng qí shǒu yǐ　希有不伤其手矣

If people don't fear death
why threaten death as a deterrent?

If people did fear death
we could seize the ones who acted strangely
and kill them

But who will do this?

There is already a great executioner
who is skilled like a master carpenter
and whoever tries to supplant the master carpenter
and carve their wood
will not escape without injuring their hands

This verse is an objection to the death penalty from ancient China. Violence begets violence. Most of us have finally understood that capital punishment is nothing more than angry revenge, and it has been repudiated in all civilized countries. Only backward countries still have the death penalty, and only backward, barbaric ones still use it regularly. The worst offenders are China, Iran, Iraq, Saudi Arabia, and the United States. Why these countries? China is a populous dictatorship that fears that its people will rise up against it. Eventually, of course, they will. Iran, Iraq, Saudi Arabia, and the United States live in fear of their religious fundamentalists. The United States also remains unable or unwilling to treat its people equally under the law. A disproportionate number of the people it murders are the descendants of the people it once enslaved. In America, murdering Black Americans casually in the night, by lynching, by assassination, by police brutality, or simply, somehow, by judicial error has always been more acceptable than murdering whites. The US government regularly commits murder on the advice of a system of law and order that it knows to be deeply flawed and biased. Thus, the United States remains a barbaric country to this day.

First of all, says Laozi, it doesn't work: *If people don't fear death, why threaten death as a deterrent?* But even if it did work, *who will do this?* Who will we ask to kill people for us?

There is an excellent farmer in northern Indiana who raises animals. He raises them for slaughter and human consumption, which for some people can never be considered ethical, but he raises them mostly outdoors, in large runs, and operates his own slaughterhouse, one of the last remaining small, independent slaughterhouses in the country. And he operates his slaughterhouse in ways that limit the suffering of the animals being killed and the people doing the killing. He once explained to me that he makes sure that nobody spends too long on the kill floor: "One person should not spend their whole working day killing," he says. "It's not good for the soul."

Killing doesn't damage only the killed but also the killer. Nature, *the master carpenter*, the Dao, the way of things, kills us all one way or another, and *whoever tries to supplant the master carpenter will not escape without injuring their hands*. Murder leaves its marks on all, whether it be a law-breaking murderer, a so-called patriot killing in a legally sanctioned war, or a murderous nation killing for hatred, fear, or revenge.

VERSE 75. SHAPE THE PATH

Outside Kombolcha, Ethiopia

75　七十五

mín zhī jǐ yǐ qí shàng shí shuì zhī duō　民之饥以其上食税之多

shì yǐ jī　是以饥

mín zhī nán zhì yǐ qí shàng zhī yǒu wéi　民之难治以其上之有为

shì yǐ nán zhì　是以难治

mín zhī qīng sǐ yǐ qí qiú shēng zhī hòu　民之轻死以其求生之厚

shì yǐ qīng sǐ　是以轻死

fū wéi wú yǐ shēng wéi zhě　夫唯无以生为者

shì xián yú guì shēng　是贤于贵生

The people are hungry
Their leaders tax them too hard
This is why they are hungry

The people are unruly
Their leaders interfere in their lives
This is why the people are unruly

The people take death lightly
They pursue life too heavily
This is why they take death lightly

Those who strive less
respect life more

You only have power over people as long as you don't take everything away from them, but when you've robbed a man of everything he's no longer in your power—he's free again.
ALEXANDR SOZHENITSYN, *THE GULAG ARCHIPELAGO*

In the last verse of a four-part treatise on tyranny, the people are at odds with their rulers. So it is, and so it has always been. Laozi says that the *people are hungry* because *their leaders tax them too hard* and that *the people are unruly* because *their leaders interfere in their lives.* How much taxation is too much taxation? How much interference is too much interference? These are perennial questions for which there is no single answer. Some will consider each solution too severe, and others will consider it too lax. The key, then, is to find an effective balance.

We seldom find balance for long and therefore engage in a constant struggle. The fight has been going on long enough to have spawned a thousand approaches and given them names: capitalism, communism, liberalism, conservatism, socialism, libertarianism, fascism. Lots of isms, but the fundamental fight—ever has been, ever will be—is between the wealthy and powerful elites and the poor and powerless masses. The wealthy and powerful must suppress or placate the masses to advance their position. The masses must unite. Society is a constant struggle between organized money and organized people.

This, of course, is the role of politics: to engage in this tugging and struggling without violence. Peace, equality, and harmony are dependent on a balanced political system. Since an equitable balance point that is optimal for a society cannot be optimal for all individuals, it is inevitable that the balance point can only be reached by people tugging from both sides. But do we have to tug so angrily, and do we have to tug from such extreme poles? Not all the blame for disunity can be placed on greedy leaders. A greedy populace—*they pursue life too heavily*—also participates. *Those who strive less respect life more.* Can we reach a healthy, vibrant, and equitable balance without so much strife?

I think Laozi would advocate a deeper, kinder approach to politics. We will always be engaged in a struggle for wealth and power, but if the battle is one that can't—and shouldn't—be permanently won and is at its best when it finds balance, maybe we can learn not to strive so hard for the more extreme political positions. Perhaps we can learn to join together, honestly and calmly, and shape the path.

VERSE 76. BEND
WITHOUT BREAKING

Longji Rice Terraces, Guangxi, China

76　七十六

rén zhī shēng yě róu ruò　人之生也柔弱

qí sǐ yě jiān qiáng　其死也坚强

cǎo mù zhī shēng yě róu cuì　草木之生也柔脆

qí sǐ yě kū gǎo　其死也枯槁

gù jiān qiáng zhě sǐ zhī tú　故坚强者死之徒

róu ruò zhě shēng zhī tú　柔弱者生之徒

shì yǐ bīng jiàng zé miè　是以兵强则灭

mù jiàng zé shé　木强则折

qiáng dà chǔ xià　强大处下

róu ruò chǔ shàng　柔弱处上

People are born supple   tender
They die rigid   stiff
Living things   grass   trees
grow pliant   sinuous
They die brittle   shriveled

So hard and stiff belong to death
and tender and gentle belong to life

Thus is the unyielding army shattered
and the unbending tree splintered

The strong and big are inferior
The soft and weak are superior

People are born supple, tender. They die rigid, stiff. What a great line. *Living things ... grow pliant, sinuous. They die brittle, shriveled.* We are a part of nature—we live as all things live and die as all things die. Life is soft and pliant. To be rigid and unyielding is to be in the thrall of death. This verse mirrors verse 36 in which *the soft and weak defeat the hard and strong,* and we are in the realms of the mighty yin again, exploring the power of yielding. *The unyielding army shattered and the unbending tree splintered.*

To bend without breaking is the secret of life, and its biggest secret, of course, is that life uses death as a revitalizing point. It never gets caught in a brittle and rigid dead end. The ancient replicators move their DNA-inscribed code from organism to organism, adapting them as necessary, discarding them as they grow brittle and shriveled, and growing new *soft, pliant, supple,* and *tender* ones. The key to life has nothing to do with the longevity of the organism and everything to do with the adaptability of the replicator.

Consider the relationship of the forest with its trees. A wildfire may seem devastating, but it may be necessary to the survival of the forest. Many forests gradually accumulate deadwood, and more deadwood means a hotter fire. Thus, an early fire that cuts quickly through a small accumulation of deadwood might affect the forest very little, while a late fire, coming to a long overmature forest, may become a wildfire. Or consider the coming and going of an ice age. The forest is pushed south ahead of the advancing ice and then dances back north, thousands of years later, following the ice as it retreats. The trees have died a billion deaths, but the forest goes on.

Or consider the Longji Rice Terraces in Guangxi Province. People moved into these remote valleys about seven hundred years ago and began to cut rice terraces. Their population grew, and the terraces climbed the mountains. A complex agricultural and irrigation system emerged and adapted its management to ever-larger rice terrace systems. Storms would damage the terraces, but the community would build them back. Culture and agriculture, mountain and terrace, and flood and drainage have persisted in an intricate adaptive dance. Soil streams off the mountain in rivulets of erosion but then is carried back onto the mountain by a stream of people with wicker baskets on their backs.

The greatest strength does not come from the things for which we use adjectives such as "strong," "hard," and "tough" but instead from resilience, the ability to bounce back and the ability to adapt. The greatest strength uses adjectives such as "yielding," "adaptable," and "regenerative.": *The strong and big are inferior. The soft and weak are superior.*

VERSE 77. NEGATIVE FEEDBACKS AND REINFORCING CYCLES

Geese

七十七

tiān zhī dào qí yóu zhāng gōng yú	天之道其犹张弓与
gāo zhě yì zhī xià zhě jǔ zhī	高者抑之下者举之
yǒu yú zhě sǔn zhī	有余者损之
bù zú zhě bù zhī	不足者补之
tiān zhī dào	天之道
sǔn yǒu yú ér bǔ bù zú	损有余而补不足
rén zhī dào	人之道
zé bù rán	则不然
sǔn bù zú yǐ fèng yǒu yú	损不足以奉有余
shú néng yǒu yú yǐ fèng tiān xià	孰能有余以奉天下
wéi yǒu dào zhě	唯有道者
shì yǐ shèng rén wéi ér bù shì	是以圣人为而不恃
gōng chéng ér bù chǔ	功成而不处
qí bù yù jiàn xián xié	其不欲见贤邪

The Way of heaven is like a stretched bow
    Its higher tip is bent down
    Its lower tip is bent up
    It takes from what has too much
    and gives to what has too little
The Way of heaven
    empties what is too full
    and fills what is too empty

The way of people is not so
    It takes from those who already have little
    and gives to those who already have much

Who has plenty and yet offers it to the world?
Only one who possesses the Dao

So the wise
    act without laying claim
    and accomplish without claiming credit
They do not flaunt their worth

Human systems are transient, despite our big brains. If only we were as smart as nature. Natural systems are deeply sustainable, and yet nature doesn't think. Meanwhile, we live in natural systems and use them to build and power our own: we are linked to them, we are of them, and yet we still fail to understand. What is it about natural systems that makes them so sustainable, and what is it about human systems that makes them so vulnerable?

The Way of heaven is like a stretched bow. It takes from what has too much and gives to what has too little. When stretched, the top of the bow bends down and the bottom bends up. Natural systems are full of self-regulating negative feedbacks that limit extremes and bring balance. *The way of people is not so. It takes from those who already have little and gives to those who already have much.* Human systems are full of destabilizing reinforcing cycles.

Natural systems are powerfully self-limiting. If a predator takes too many prey, the resulting lack of food will limit the predator's numbers. If a parasite evolves greater virulence, resistance will likely evolve in its host. When a forest burns in a wildfire, the newly opened, fertilized land will soon flush with new growth. These self-balancing cycles are negative feedbacks, and they resemble the thermostat in your house. When the temperature of your house climbs, the air conditioner turns on and the temperature is brought back under control.

A reinforcing cycle is a positive feedback, like a thermostat malfunction. The house temperature climbs, but instead of the air conditioner turning on, the heater turns on. The house gets even hotter, the thermostat sends another signal, and the temperature spirals out of control. Natural systems almost never do this (notable exceptions are in the era of anthropogenic climate change: warming melts arctic ice, reducing albedo and causing warming; warming melts permafrost, releasing methane-causing warming), but human systems do it all the time. Capitalism has the tendency to steal from the poor and give to the rich. Rich countries extract resources from poor countries, at gunpoint if necessary. The poor pay more for groceries in food deserts and are stuck with higher interest rates on their credit cards. Having money—capital—is very lucrative, and poverty can be a trap. Welfare systems can redress the balance, but the imbalance itself is systemic.

But while human economic systems can find equilibrium points between rich and poor, they fail to find balance with the environment. Politics is a squabble among humans for the resources of the earth. A serious political system that might protect Earth from human squabbling has yet to be found. *Who has plenty and yet offers it to the world? Only one who possesses the Dao.*

VERSE 78. THE PERSISTENCE OF WATER

Bahia de Cochinos (Bay of Pigs), Cuba

78 七十八

tiān xià mò róu ruò yú shuǐ 天下莫柔弱于水

ér gōng jiān qiáng zhě mò zhī néng shèng 而攻坚强者莫之能胜

yǐ qí wú yǐ yì zhī 以其无以易之

ruò zhī shèng jiàng 弱之胜强

róu zhī shèng gāng 柔之胜刚

tiān xià mò bù zhī mò néng xíng 天下莫不知莫能行

shì yǐ shèng rén yún 是以圣人云

shòu guó zhī gòu shì wèi shè jì zhǔ 受国之垢是谓社稷主

shòu guó bù xiáng shì wéi tiān xià wáng 受国不祥是为天下王

zhēng yán ruò fǎn 正言若反

Nothing is softer or gentler than water
and yet nothing is more potent
for attacking the hard and rough
Nothing can match it

Soft gets the better of hard
Gentle gets the better of rough

Everybody knows this
    and yet none practices it

So the wise say
Bear the nation's humiliations
    to become worthy of its fertile soil
    and abundant harvests
Bear the nation's misfortunes
    to become a lord of the world

True words seem false

This is the fourth verse focused on the persistent soft power of water. Verse 8 asked us to be as humble as water. Verse 43 asked us to be like water, like air—a yin force that would patiently grind down the strength of yang materials, as with rocks. Verse 66 showed us that humble water, flowing to the lowest place, was the force that would give the valley shape. Here, Laozi reminds us of this central theme: *Nothing is softer or gentler than water and yet nothing is more potent.* As we reach the end of the book, we are returned for a last reiteration of the superiority of yin power over yang as illustrated by water. *Soft gets the better of hard. Gentle gets the better of rough.*

Meanwhile, a hint of frustration creeps in. We have heard this before from Laozi, as if he's yelling at us: "Come on. Wake up! This is not complicated, people!" *The Way is broad,* and it is *flat and straight* (v. 53). *My words are easily understood . . . and yet none seem to . . . follow them* (v. 70). Here, he says that *everybody knows this, and yet none practices it.*

How might we emulate the persistence of water? Life presents us with an abundance of opportunities to test our persistence. We must *bear the nation's humiliations* and its *misfortunes.* Our nation will suffer ups and downs, but we must be in it for the long haul. We cannot be the rats that are the first to abandon the sinking ship; we must hang on in there through thick and thin and show persistence. We must help to build and rebuild. We must teach and reteach and, if necessary, reteach again. Only through such patience and persistence will we be worthy of the nation's fertile soil and abundant harvests. In the United Sates in 2025, this is a very important message. It looks like the brownshirts are coming, and perhaps it is time to get the hell out of here, but as the Sufis say, "At the end of the world, plant a tree."

Laozi ends with one of his enigmatic closing phrases. Do you remember *By this* (vv. 21 and 54); *They reject that. They accept this* (vv. 12 and 38); and *They let go of that and choose this* (v. 72)? Here he ends with *True words seem false.* I think he is urging us to be alert for the counterintuitive. It seems ridiculous that water should be so powerful, and so Laozi urges us to look closer. *True words seem false*—but look closer. No situation, however hopeless it may seem, warrants giving up. Keep going, keep teaching, keep offering kindness and compassion: hold on. *Nothing is softer or gentler than water and yet nothing is more potent. Everybody knows this and yet none practices it.*

VERSE 79. DE-ESCALATION

Koi

79　七十九

hé dà yuàn bì yǒu yú yuàn　和大怨必有余怨

ān kě yǐ wéi shàn　安可以为善

shì yǐ shèng rén zhí zuǒ qì　是以圣人执左契

ér bù zé yú rén　而不责于人

yǒu dé sī qì　有德司契

wú dé sī chè　无德司彻

tiān dào wú qīn　天道无亲

cháng yú shàn rén　常与善人

When bitter rivals make peace
some grievances are likely to linger
How to manage this?

The wise keep their part of the deal
but don't insist on all their rights

It is virtue to attend to your own obligations
It is not virtue to insist others do the same

The Way of heaven does not play favorites
but it does favor goodness

There are some real gems at the end of the book. Here, Laozi makes an important commentary on the power of restraint. The bitter rivals discussed in this verse might be warring nations, but they might also be coworkers or feuding lovers. How should we behave when we resolve a conflict with a rival? *Some grievances are likely to linger. How to manage this?* Laozi asks us to keep our obligations while forgiving our rivals theirs. This, of course, is not easy. We tend to feel cheated even when we shouldn't, and when we feel cheated we tend to act selfishly. We are exquisitely alert to the faults of others but stubbornly blind to our own—we have a powerful sense of self-righteousness. It is hard for us to see when we're wrong in a rivalry, harder still to admit it and hardest of all to act generously.

As an example, consider the crisis of trust between Black Americans and the police in the United States. High-profile police murders of Black men caught on video escalated this crisis to the national conscious with the murder of George Floyd in Minneapolis on May 25, 2020, and we reached a tipping point. How do we move forward in a way that can heal the volatile divide between African Americans and the police? Well, we need to reform the police, and we need to recognize that *grievances will linger*. America has always suppressed, dishonored, and murdered Black men. So, the onus is on the nation to keep its part of the deal as a society. We need to *attend to our own obligations* as a nation and *not insist others do the same*. America needs to de-escalate unilaterally.

In the everyday, the simple advice comes in two parts. First is the easy part: fulfill your obligations unselfishly. Second is the difficult part: let the rest of it go. You may expect to get burned, and sometimes you will, but things will often work out better than you expected. Either way, the anger and conflict will be reduced. This doesn't mean that you shouldn't remind Honey that it is his job to do the dishes or her job to do the laundry; just don't carry it with you. The idea is to employ de-escalation by example. It is okay to go first with kindness and go it alone with trust.

And what will be the result of your unilateral disarmament? *The Way of heaven does not play favorites.* Your kindness may not be reciprocated, and you may get taken advantage of from time to time. *But it does favor goodness.* The approach will generally bring out the best in others, to everybody's benefit, and the calmness and equanimity you will find will more than make up for the occasions when you get burned.

VERSE 80. UTOPIA

Village in rural Guangxi

80 八十

xiǎo guó guǎ mín	小国寡民
shǐ yǒu shén bó zhī qì ér bù yòng	使有什伯之器而不用
shǐ mín chóng sǐ ér bù yuǎn xǐ	使民重死而不远徙
suī yǒu zhōu yú wú suǒ chéng zhī	虽有舟舆无所乘之
suī yǒu jiǎ bīng wú suǒ chén zhī	虽有甲兵无所陈之
shǐ mín fù jiē shéng ér yòng zhī	使民复结绳而用之
gān qí shí měi qí fú	甘其食美其服
ān qí jū lè qí sú	安其居乐其俗
lín guó xiāng wàng	邻国相望
jī quǎn zhī shēng xiāng wén	鸡犬之声相闻
mín zhì lǎo sǐ bù xiāng wǎng lái	民至老死不相往来

Imagine a small country with few citizens

It is well equipped with tools
    but few of them are used
The people take death seriously
    and do not roam
There are boats and carts
    but they are seldom ridden
They have armor and weapons
    but feel no need to display them
They have even returned to using knotted cords
    in place of writing

Their food is nutritious
Their clothes are comfortable
Their customs are cheerful

Other nations are very close
    Dogs can be heard barking
    Roosters can be heard crowing

But imagine these people
They can grow old
and die
without feeling any need to explore

This verse pops up out of nowhere, as if, nearing the end of the book, someone has asked Laozi, "So, what would life look like if we were to do all these things you advise?" Here is his sketch. He conjures a small country with few people. In my mind, it is a green valley of rich soils pockmarked with little villages of modest wood houses, rice paddies, and animal pens surrounded by wooded slopes. It has everything you could need but is simple and unadorned. People don't invite trouble; they live calmly. They stroll everywhere, even though there are boats and carts, because they are never in a hurry. There is no army and no bureaucracy. The food and clothing are simple but of superior quality. It is a lovely little bucolic paradise with quaint customs. It is Laozi's vision of utopia.

It may not be your idea of utopia. You might even recoil at the very idea of utopia. Our society has a rich history of great literature about societies that began as wannabe utopias but ended up as dystopias—George Orwell's *1984*, Lois Lowry's *The Giver*, and Margaret Atwood's *The Handmaid's Tale* come to mind.[23] And we are well aware that some of the worst political failures of the twentieth century, the communist revolutions that collapsed into oppressive dictatorships, were originally seen by many as visionary candidate utopias.

Contrast this vision of utopia with a modern equivalent, which might be exemplified by the question "If you had three wishes . . . ?" What do people wish for? Well, we all vary, of course, but we often wish for wealth and stuff. Or consider the question "If you won the lottery . . . ?" Many people have won the lottery, and research shows that an inordinate number of them burned their newfound wealth on stuff and ended up more miserable than before.

The key characteristic of Laozi's utopia is that it lacks stuff. His utopia is based on peace and quiet, self-sufficiency, and community. What would Laozi wish for if he had three wishes? I like to think he'd just ask for less.

That the people in Laozi's utopia are happy is evidenced by the fact that they don't want to leave. They don't even feel the need to explore despite the fact that *other nations are close*, so close that *they can hear the dogs barking and roosters crowing*.

And another interpretation of a community that lives simply *without feeling the need to explore* is that Laozi may be speaking out against military adventurism and colonization. Just stay in your own valley, tend your own fields, and build your own community. And let others do same.

VERSE 81. WISDOM
OVER KNOWLEDGE

Half Dome, Yosemite National Park, California

81 八十一

xìn yán bù měi	信言不美
měi yán bù xìn	美言不信
shàn zhě bù biàn	善者不辩
biàn zhě bù shàn	辩者不善
zhī zhě bù bó	知者不博
bó zhě bù zhī	博者不知
shèng rén bù jī	圣人不积
jì yǐ wéi rén jǐ yù yǒu	既以为人己愈有
jì yǐ yú rén jǐ yù duō	既以与人己愈多
tiān zhī dào lì ér bù hài	天之道利而不害
shèng rén zhī dào wéi ér bù zhēng	圣人之道为而不争

Truthful words are not pretty
Pretty words are not true

Good people are not argumentative
Contentious people are not good

Wise people are not learned
Learned people are not wise

The wise do not hoard
    but by serving others receive more
    and by giving to others gain more

The Way of heaven
    is to help without harming
The Way of the wise
    is to serve without competing

The closing chapter of the *Daodejing* presents a roundup of the virtues, a summary of the De. This chapter reminds us to be moderate, humble, and honest and to live up to the ideal of the Dao. First, we tackle the dangers of false speech: *Truthful words are not pretty. Pretty words are not true.* We should be wary of deceivers who promise things they cannot provide, and we too should be cautious when making promises. A good indication of dishonesty is the tendency to argue. Your words will stand for themselves if they are true, so Laozi adds that *good people are not argumentative.* They do not contend. The desire to win arguments is one of the desires that Laozi repeatedly warns us about. You don't usually win much when you win an argument. It is much more effective to communicate without contention.

This brings us to the learned. With the statement *wise people are not learned* and *learned people are not wise*, Laozi reminds us that there is a vast difference between knowledge and wisdom.

Here's the thing. A substantial part of society has grown tired of its experts and turned on them. Around the time of the Brexit vote for the United Kingdom's exit from the European Union, Michael Gove, a leading Brexiteer said, "I think the people of this country have had enough of experts." Donald Trump didn't need experts to know, thanks to his bigly intuition, that the coronavirus would infect about fifteen people in the United States and then "like a miracle, *disappear.*" The antiexpert madness smacks of a conspiracy theory.

But the experts do share some of the blame. Knowledge can be a problem if it comes without wisdom. Experts might be deeply knowledgeable of their own narrow field but ignorant of the broader implications of their conclusions. Yes, it makes sense to control weeds in crop fields, but do we need to spray the entire landscape with herbicides? Yes, wood can be a sustainable product, but have you noticed what's happening to our forests? Yes, police should have the equipment they need, but do they need to be equipped like an army? Yes, medical science can save and enhance the quality of lives—vaccines, aseptic surgery, pain relief—but gene-edited humans? Come on, man.

Deep knowledge and highly refined skill are wonderful things and valuable, but they only reach their potential when applied with wisdom. Specialized knowledge too often causes experts to reach for their own Maslow's Hammer:[24] "To a man with a hammer, everything looks like a nail." Cleverness is necessary to develop a thing. Wisdom may show that it shouldn't be used.

As often is the case in the *Daodejing*, the verse ends by returning to the simple question: Are you acting in harmony with the Dao? *The Way of heaven is to help without harming*, and *the Way of the wise is to serve without competing.* Ask yourself what would Laozi do? The answer is simple: Be happy. Be kind. Is all.

NOTES

1. Burton Watson, *Records of the Grand Historian of China*, 2nd ed. (Columbia University Press, 1993).
2. Robert G. Henricks, *Lao-Tzu Te-Tao Ching: A New Translation Based on the Recently Discovered Ma-wang-tui Texts* (Ballantine Books, 1989).
3. Robert G. Henricks, *Lao Tzu's Tao Te Ching: A Translation of the Startling New Documents Found at Guodian* (Columbia University Press, 2000).
4. James Miller, *Daoism: A Short Introduction* (Oneworld, 2003).
5. Livia Kohn, *Daoism and Chinese Culture* (Three Pines, 2001).
6. David Keightley, *The Ancestral Landscape: Time, Space, and Community in Shang Dynasty China, ca. 1200–1045 B.C.* (University of California Press, 2000).
7. The assignment of masculinity to yang and femininity to yin is taken in the sense in which it would have likely been understood at the time, not in the more comprehensive way we think of sex and gender today.
8. Aldo Leopold, *A Sand County Almanac* (Oxford University Press, 1949).
9. Wendell Berry, "The Contrariness of the Mad Farmer," in *The Selected Poems of Wendell Berry* (Counterpoint, 1999).
10. James Lovelock, *Gaia: A New Look at Life on Earth* (Oxford University Press, 1979).
11. Alwyn D. Rees, *Life in a Welsh Countryside* (University of Wales Press, 1950).
12. The voice of Frank Oz, first appearing in *The Phantom Menace* (directed by George Lucas and produced by Rick McCallum for Lucasfilm, Ltd., 1999).
13. Douglas Adams, *The Hitchhiker's Guide to the Galaxy* (Pan Books, 1979).
14. Alan Watts, *Tao: The Watercourse Way* (Pantheon, 1975).
15. *The Matrix* (directed by the Wachawskis and produced by Joel Silver for Warner Bros. Pictures, 1999).
16. Albert Woodfox, *Solitary: Unbroken by Four Decades in Solitary Confinement; My Story of Transformation and Hope* (Grove Atlantic, 2019).
17. Claimed variously as an African proverb, but the origins are unclear.
18. Dan Harris, *10% Happier: How I Tamed the Voice in My Head, Reduced Stress without Losing My Edge, and Found Self-Help That Actually Works—A True Story* (It Books, 2014).
19. Donald Hebb, *The Organization of Behavior: A Neuropsychological Theory* (Wiley, 1949).
20. David Graeber, *Bullshot Jobs: A Theory* (Simon & Schuster, 2018).

21. *When We Were Kings* (directed by Leon Gast and produced by Leon Gast, David Sonenberg, and Taylor Hackford for Polygram, 1996).

22. Aleksandr Solzhenitsyn, *The Gulag Archipelago: An Experiment in Literary Investigation* (YMCA Press, 1973).

23. George Orwell, *1984* (Secker & Warburg, 1949); Lois Lowry, *The Giver* (Houghton Mifflin, 1993); and Margaret Atwood, *The Handmaid's Tale* (McClelland & Stewart, 1985).

24. Abraham H. Maslow, *The Psychology of Science: A Reconnaissance* (Harper & Row, 1966).

INDEX

Page numbers in italics indicate Figures.

ABOUT THE AUTHOR

Steve Hallett is a professor of horticulture at Purdue University and teaches classes on sustainability, environmental science, and food justice. He is the cofounder of the Purdue University Student Farm and the Sustainable Food and Farming Systems degree program. Hallett is an award-winning teacher listed in Purdue's Book of Great Teachers and a member of its Teaching Academy. He is the author of *Life Without Oil, The Efficiency Trap, A Life for a Life*, and *Ancient Wisdoms for Modern Crises: Learning from Laozi's "Daodejing."*

www.ingramcontent.com/pod-product-compliance
Lightning Source LLC
Chambersburg PA
CBHW051949270326
41929CB00015B/2582